ABOUT THE AUTHOR

Susanna Abse has been a psychoanalytic psychotherapist for over 30 years. She specialises in helping couples and was CEO of the charity Tavistock Relationships from 2006 to 2016 and Chair of the British Psychoanalytic Council from 2018 to 2021.

Alongside her professional writing on couples therapy, she has contributed articles on wider social and political issues to the *Guardian*, the *New Statesman* and *Open Democracy*. In 2019, she presented a series of films called *Britain on the Couch* for Channel 4 News. She is co-editor of The Library of Couple and Family Psychoanalysis for Routledge Books and is a trustee of the Freud Museum, London.

tell me
the truth
about
love

tell me the truth about love

13 Tales from the Therapist's Couch

SUSANNA ABSE

EBURY
PRESS

1

Ebury Press, an imprint of Ebury Publishing,
20 Vauxhall Bridge Road,
London SW1V 2SA

Ebury Press is part of the Penguin Random House group of companies
whose addresses can be found at global.penguinrandomhouse.com

 Penguin
Random House
UK

First published in the United Kingdom by Ebury Press in 2022

www.penguin.co.uk

A CIP catalogue record for this book is available from the British Library

ISBN 9781529107333

Printed and bound in Great Britain by Clays Ltd, Elcograf S.p.A.

The authorised representative in the EEA is Penguin Random House Ireland,
Morrison Chambers, 32 Nassau Street, Dublin D02 YH68

Penguin Random House is committed to a sustainable future
for our business, our readers and our planet. This book is made
from Forest Stewardship Council® certified paper.

MIX
Paper from
responsible sources
FSC
www.fsc.org   FSC® C018179

For Paul, my fellow truth seeker.

We do as we have been done by.

—John Bowlby

CONTENTS

INTRODUCTION

The couple relationship is at the centre of this book, just as it is at the centre of our lives. We are born wanting to reach out and relate to others, and each of us, whilst not necessarily growing up with two parents, has a deep internal structure rooted in the idea of intimate connection. Despite technological advances, there is always a sperm and an egg, a nipple and a mouth – two bodies and two minds coming together. For humans, we cannot make babies single-handed and even if we could, the drive for 'intercourse' and human interaction would remain. We are hardwired for love.

This sense of connection lies at the heart of many of our dreams and fantasies and drives the narrative of fairy tales, which Carl Jung believed revealed something about the basis of human nature. It is for this reason that I have written this book in the form of a series of psychoanalytic allegories, with fairy tale-like titles, through which I try to shed light on some of the universal themes and eternal dilemmas we face in relationships, and which draw couples together and, all too often, tear them apart.

The longing for transformation is at the heart of what often brings people to therapy, just as it is at the heart of the fairy tale, where a happy outcome is achieved only after the central character overcomes huge obstacles and adversity. Clearly, psychotherapy doesn't transform the frog into a prince; however, it does attempt to take the patient on a journey where they come to understand that the frog and the prince are two halves of the same person and 'transformation' perhaps then comes from accepting this. Yet some patients seek a quick fix – a magic potion – and are disappointed when they find that there isn't one.

The case histories in this book are inspired and informed by more than 35 years of practice and tens of thousands of sessions with many hundreds of living, breathing patients. The importance of any patient feeling safe in the knowledge that what they tell me is confidential means that I haven't written about any specific individuals. Readers will ask, 'But then are these stories true?' The answer is that they are 'true' in the same way that fairy tales are 'true'. They aim to tell a deeper truth about the human condition. Each chapter tells a story that represents problems and patterns of behaviour I have witnessed in different forms over and over again. Though they are not about any specific patient they offer truths about the human need for others and the reality of our vulnerability, about the inevitability of dependence and the fear of it.

When exploring love relationships, it's vital to question what *is* truth? Philosophers describe truth as that which accords with reality, but reality is subjective: my reality will be different from yours and yours from mine. I point this out because this question goes to the heart of couple therapy. In treatment, many discover that not only have they hidden the truth from others but that they have also been lying to themselves – because being honest with oneself usually means facing up to painful truths which we often avoid. Thus, there are two aspects to 'truth' between a couple: the first involves facing one's own feelings and knowing about your own experiences; the second involves facing your partner's feelings and understanding *their* experience. The challenge is whether these two truths can co-exist without one threatening to obliterate the other.

Most couples take a little time to become curious – to become interested in how their inner truth may not reflect some objective reality but is, at least in part, a reflection of their own family experience. But when partners do become curious, less defensive and open up about their feelings, they can rediscover each other and a different kind of truth emerges – one that is shared and which creates a new narrative. This is not simply an intellectual or cognitive knowing but rather an emotional process. As Jung said, 'We should not pretend to understand the world only by intellect. We apprehend it just as much by *feeling*. The judgement of the intellect is only part of the truth.'*

Jung was wise – as a psychotherapist, I have learnt that all our experience is suffused with and shaped by our previous experiences. We approach every new event or relationship full of preconceptions – we are never free of these influences; though we may imagine ourselves to be impartial, objective witnesses to our lives, we are not. The past lives on in the present.

In couple therapy, then, the aim is to seek truth – but not to possess it. Rather it is a process of unfolding something between a couple that leads to discoveries which in turn lead to understanding and, sometimes, to transformation. I hope that in writing this book I may help readers reach a deeper and richer insight into themselves and their own relationships. Couple therapy is largely about getting to know things about yourself and your partner that have been hidden from view behind our assumptions. It's about letting go of one set of 'truths' and becoming open to a more shared understanding of each other – that is the truth about love.

* Carl Jung, *Psychological Types*, epilogue (Routledge, 2017).

PART ONE
FRAGILE BONDS

We are never so defenceless as when we love.
  —Sigmund Freud, *Civilization and Its Discontents*

All humans are fragile, though we may spend a lifetime pretending we are not. We are born helpless and that experience of helplessness is not forgotten. It echoes through our lives and disturbs us in the dead of night when our grown-up selves are sleeping.

Our only real protection from human fragility is other humans. Humans with hands that lift us; humans with arms that hold us; humans with minds that understand us. Without that, we are alone – and no human is designed for that. But other humans also threaten us; they remind us of the times we were dropped, when the arms weren't gently holding but roughly constraining and take us back to the times we were misunderstood. So, when it comes to love, we armour ourselves against this fragility because we are afraid.

VICTORIA AND RUPERT REFUSE TO COME OUT OF THE DOLL'S HOUSE

Some couples are shockingly childish. They bicker and fight, snap and wail, and like nothing better than having an audience to win over to their side. Once they've exhausted all their friends then a couple therapist often comes in handy!

I have colleagues who work only with individuals and insist they'd never want to work with a couple because they'd feel so irritated with the rowing. I remember many years ago teaching a seminar and a student therapist getting very cross with the case material I was presenting. Exasperated, they asked, 'For goodness' sake, why don't they just call it a day if they can't get on?' It brought a brief round of applause and nodding of student heads.

We may disapprove of couples bickering or behaving like children, yet it seems to me that couples become couples partly because an intimate relationship is one of the only ways it's acceptable for adults to regress. Where else can we talk in silly voices? Call and be called 'pudding pie' and suchlike? Who else can you throw water at or even ketchup in a play fight? Who else will read to you? Sing to you? Hold you and caress you? It is perhaps one of life's paradoxes that it's the norm for parents to share the warmth of a bed, whilst children, once past early infancy, are trained to sleep alone. Being a couple lets us return to this world of play and touch, which is generally barred to us in the rest of our adult lives.

Nearly all intimate love relationships have childlike qualities: we use baby words of love with each other and snuggle, stroke and play. Love-making itself offers the opportunity to stroke and caress and suck and tickle and explore in a way that most of adult life doesn't. Recently, on a beach in Greece I watched a couple sticking grass stalks up each other's noses – testing how long they could each bear it. Rolling with laughter, I observed how completely in love they were and how much they were bonded by their childishness.

But despite knowing this, I have to confess that there are some couples whose infantile behaviour is so regressive and destructive that it becomes hard to bear, even for an old hand like me.

Victoria and Rupert were extremely hard going. They were in their late thirties and beautiful, rich and clever but, I repeat, extremely hard going. Both could be disarmingly charming on their own but together they were a nightmare. So many dinner parties ruined, holidays disrupted and tearful phone conversations late at night had led to their friends drawing a line through their names and so they turned up in my consulting room, ready to put me through a similar experience.

I, however, having endured many hours listening to similarly warring couples, knew I had to take a different approach. There were tantrums and tears in the sessions and I received histrionic phone calls and emails between appointments, where each would forward me texts or emails that had passed between them. Sometimes I'd be copied into these exchanges and asked to adjudicate as if I was the giver of justice. Both convinced of their rightness, they would appeal to me with tear-filled eyes to validate their point of view. They'd come to each session having not spoken to each other for several days and then, each Thursday in my office, would eventually make up and leave my room together laughing and smiling like a pair of naughty children.

There are some couples who, when in the middle of a row, voice their outrage at what they feel are unfair accusations and distortions of truth meted out by their partner. 'If only I'd had a video running, it would prove me right. It just didn't happen like that!' they scream, each of them seeing everything through their own lens – a lens that is distorted and shaped by past experiences, which often include trauma, neglect and abuse. And this introduces confusion, making it hard to distinguish feeling from facts. The angrier and more upset partners get, the more assumptions are made about the motives and intentions of the other.

I hoped, with careful work, Victoria and Rupert might break out of this cycle and begin to become curious. Curious about themselves and curious about each other. The assumptions they made about each other, together with the excitement they created to avoid feeling sad, left them repeating a cycle of anger, betrayal and passionate reconciliation over and over again. And whilst it sometimes seemed they were excited by it, I could see that, underneath the noise, they felt desperation and despair at never feeling understood or safe. I knew if anything was going to change, they needed to get depressed, they needed to recognise that their relationship wasn't a doll's house where the furniture could be thrown about and the figures tipped upside down with no consequences or damage. I wanted them to feel how serious and sad this was. I wanted them to talk about their fears. I wanted them, in short, to be different.

Whether I was right to want all this is highly questionable. Should a psychotherapist have such clear goals for their patients? Isn't it our job to facilitate what our patients want, not what we desire for them? I knew this, of course, so how was I to survive the frustrations of working with Victoria and Rupert? How was I to bear the endless sessions of petty fighting and rapturous reconciliation? And when, as my exasperated student rightly asked, is it time to call it a day?

I found myself thinking back to another couple who I'd seen many years earlier. Roly and Clive were very young when they came, just 23 and 24. They too had passionate ups and downs, breaking up and reconciling repeatedly. The slightest thing would trigger mutual threats to end the relationship and I'd never know what to expect from week to week. I'd sternly encourage them to take the work with me seriously but it seemed impossible and after several weeks of no-shows, unpaid bills and frantic texts, I suggested in an email that perhaps they weren't ready to settle down to therapy and that they should contact me when they felt they could commit.

How ironic. Commitment was of course the very problem Roly and Clive were struggling with. Both felt too scared to really pledge themselves to the relationship and both found it impossible to commit to the therapy.

Was this, I wondered, Victoria and Rupert's problem too? They were a fair bit older than Roly and Clive and the stakes were therefore considerably higher. On the other hand, they had the financial resources to play these games with each other, in ever more dramatic ways.

One grey Tuesday in February, I struggled into work with a streaming cold. Victoria and Rupert were the last appointment of the day and I, exhausted, secretly hoped they might cancel so I could go home and get into my PJs. Six o'clock came and went, and I was beginning to think about getting my coat when, fifteen minutes late, the buzzer went. They entered with a flurry, unzipping their matching Moncler down jackets and, without taking a breath, launched into their latest drama.

It seemed they'd been skiing over a long weekend in Zermatt and on the second day Victoria had taken umbrage over Rupert's provocative comment that her bum did indeed look big in her salopettes. She'd instantly hired a car and driven for five hours to meet friends skiing in St Moritz. Ordinary mortals would have had to stay put and work it out but, being impulse driven and rich, she didn't need to. She could make her point in the most dramatic way, leaving Rupert alone on the side of the mountain.

This kind of 'acting out' is very anti-therapeutic. Therapy is about sitting with things, bearing feelings, tolerating discomfort, facing our fears. Victoria and Rupert seemed deeply committed to not committing to this process.

There was, however, one thing they both wanted more than anything else and when I spoke about this in the sessions they'd go quiet and still as my words reverberated through them, echoing their oceanic desire to start a family. To be a family. Something neither of them had had when growing up. I won't detail their individual backgrounds. You, the reader, can, I'm sure, imagine the circumstances of the neglect they'd suffered. Lots of money and very little care. Sent young to grand boarding schools. Many treats that hadn't compensated for a lack of real attention and love. Lots of holidays and big gestures but no stability. It was very painful if you stopped for two minutes to think about it. Which is exactly what they didn't or couldn't do.

In the sessions, as the weeks went by, there were repeated damaging break-ups and make-ups. I'd be firm and stop them bickering and then I'd try to connect them to how sad this all was. How sad that they'd missed each other for three days when they'd planned to go to the theatre or to Paris, Rome or Zermatt. Every cancelled event or spoilt occasion. I'd speak to the waste of it all and the waste of their deepest hopes and gradually, very gradually, they began to thaw, to show genuine sadness and to turn back to each other sooner after each argument than had previously been the case.

Children love a doll's house; it's a place where fantasy can dominate and where the child can be all-powerful and in control. Victoria and Rupert, who were so fragile inside, liked to pretend they were unbreakable but of course they were not.

Rows between couples are inevitable. Differences are not only inevitable, but important. Perhaps more essential than agreement is the working through of our differences, so that we really find each other. You are not me. I am not you. And yes, that is difficult and disappointing but also interesting and sometimes exciting. And if we are just a 'we', then who am I?

So, the trick of being a happy-enough couple isn't to have no rows but to learn to make up well and to repair the relationship. Rupert and Victoria made up quickly enough in the early days of therapy but they never repaired anything, never learnt anything. It was manic repair to avoid feeling, to avoid thinking and to avoid knowing about their pain.

JACK AND JILL TUMBLE DOWN THE HILL

Jack Sprat could eat no fat,
His wife could eat no lean;
And so betwixt them both,
They lick'd the platter clean.
                    —Nursery rhyme

Marriage and long-term partnerships can help us to develop and grow. The nurture and, indeed, the frustration that we encounter in our relationships help us mature. So when a couple comes to therapy, it's often because this maturing process has got stuck or frozen and the couple, rather than finding their relationship helps them to flourish, instead find themselves trapped in patterns of destructive feelings and behaviour. Couple psychotherapy can unblock this, launching the couple back into a more creative journey through the life cycle of having children, raising and then launching them; developing careers; nurturing friendships; managing retirement and, of course, in time, facing old age and death. For some couples, whose relationship hasn't matured, this frozen or stuck state has come about because of the avoidance of all conflict.

I remember an early case, perhaps 30 years ago, which first brought this home to me. Both were artists and they lived in the countryside, in a quiet, isolated place, though it was not far from London. I shall call them Jack and Jill. They were an older couple with no children and no desire for children. As I got to know them, I concluded that the reason for this was that they still felt like children themselves; babes lost in the woods.

At that time, I was a fresh-faced trainee therapist working in the building of a large NHS clinic. It wasn't a particularly friendly place but I was keen to follow the many rules about conducting appointments. In this clinic, the protocol was that when patients arrived, I had to phone down to an indifferent receptionist who would then send the couple up to my office, three floors above.

It was a Tuesday afternoon and I'd spent the morning in seminars and with my supervisor, preparing for a new couple. I closed the office window, looked at my watch and saw it was 2pm so I rang down to see if they'd arrived. The receptionist informed me the couple were here and were now on their way up. I knew nothing much about Jack and Jill but waited with anticipation by the lift to greet them and escort them to my room. The minutes ticked by and, as I watched the hands of the clock move gradually towards ten minutes past two, I began to wonder where they'd got to.

Then, turning to the adjacent stairs, I could see an older couple slowly hauling their way up to where I was waiting. I wasn't sure if this was Jack and Jill, so we stood there slightly awkwardly until I said, 'Hello, I'm Susanna Abse. Are you here to see me?' They nodded and silently followed me down the corridor towards my sparsely furnished office with its clinical linoleum floor and metal windows.

By the time I reached the door, the couple were lagging some 20 feet behind me. Admittedly, I'd walked briskly but their pace was snail-like and once inside, it seemed to take an age for them to dispense with their bags and coats and settle themselves.

I introduced myself properly and told them we had until 3.15pm and that this was a consultation to explore whether couple psychotherapy might be helpful for them. And then I asked them to tell me a little about why they'd come.

There was a long pause and I took this opportunity to study them closely. Jack was tall and very thin, and I thought that once he would have been very handsome. His hair was splattered with grey and looked like it hadn't seen a comb for some months.

Jill also looked a bit uncared for in a baggy tweed skirt and thick, dark tights that had seen better days. She wore an impressive orange bead necklace and her hair, which was pinned in a loose bun, was dyed scarlet red. I could see her white roots as she bent to place her bag on the blue lino beside her and as she straightened up, she looked at me and gave a small, warm smile.

The silence continued but eventually, Jack, looking anxiously at Jill, broke the silence.

'We've been having trouble with our neighbours.' He stopped and I nodded encouragingly for him to continue.

Again, he glanced at Jill before slowly explaining that their neighbours were objecting to a new studio they'd built on their land. I felt perplexed but curious – this was certainly an unusual subject to open with. Jack described how the studio, though far from their nearest neighbours, was on the side of a hill and therefore very visible. Their neighbours were complaining that the building spoiled the view and had now written to the local planning authorities, who'd informed them that they should have got permission before building. They were very worried, Jack continued, as they feared they were going to have to tear it down. I could sense the anxiety emanating off him.

Jill frowned but said nothing, so I prodded a little and asked if this concern was causing difficulties between them.

Again, there was a long silence before, once again, Jack took the lead. 'Maybe,' he said.

I turned to Jill. 'I wonder if you wanted to say anything further, Jill. Perhaps you see things differently?' Little did I know then that this question went to the heart of their problem. Could she see things differently? Apparently not.

Although Jack and Jill seemed hesitant to discuss any problems between them, they did tell me a little more about their lives. They'd met on their first day at art school, both new to London and quite overwhelmed by it all. Jack said he was attracted to Jill's serenity; she seemed so calm and composed – 'Zen-like'. Jill said that she'd been struck by how tall Jack was; he seemed like the strong and silent type, which reminded her of her brother. They talked animatedly about how they'd developed a way of working together that had been central to the making of their art. Inseparable since they were 18, they were now in their late fifties. They made me think of the artists Gilbert and George – a heterosexual version of that couple, two peas in a creative pod. Their work had clearly been the driving force of their existence and Jill spoke at some length about what a wonderful sculptor Jack was and how much she tried to emulate his work ethic, though sometimes she found that quite challenging. She smiled broadly and laughed as she said this and he laughed expansively too, though I couldn't really make out what was funny. As the session went on, I noticed that both of them laughed and smiled a great deal. Was this a way of covering up more uncomfortable feelings?

After they left, I wrote 'Babes in the wood?' on my notepad, which was my shorthand for a particular kind of couple who find any conflict or differences particularly challenging and will do anything to keep things smooth and harmonious between them. As a result, all the conflict and difficulties happen with people outside the little couple world, with in-laws or siblings or, perhaps, neighbours. I had the sense that Jack and Jill were trying to live in a kind of childlike refuge, buried in the countryside away from the intrusions and demands of the outside world. The only blot on the horizon seemed to be their neighbours, who they feared were out to get them.

'Babes in the wood' couples try to create a relationship where partners, like good mothers, apprehend and meet each other's needs in a complete, almost unspoken way. Each partner adapts to the other so that there is an illusion of oneness which can feel like a blissful experience of being held and secure.

> You and I
> Have so much love
> That it
> Burns like fire,
> In which we bake a lump of clay
> Moulded into a figure of you.
> And a figure of me.
> Then we take both of them,
> And break them into pieces,
> And mix the pieces with water,
> And mould again a figure of you,
> And a figure of me.
> I am in your clay
> You are in my clay
> In life we share a single quilt.
> In death we will share one coffin
> —Kuan Tao-Sheng, 'Married Love'

This poem speaks to that wonderful feeling of oneness that most love affairs begin with. When we fall in love and place our heart in someone's hands – which is, after all, quite a risky thing to do with a stranger – feeling completely fused together gives an illusion of security. Unconsciously, we believe, 'If we are one – you can't hurt me. If we are the same, locked forever in a loving embrace, you'll never leave me.'

In most relationships, adult partners go through a gradual disillusionment and separation process. Life happens and the honeymoon ends. Suddenly you're living not with this ideal person but with someone more real, with their own point of view and their own separate needs. This disillusionment can herald the end of a relationship or it can be the start of a new phase. Usually, it feels like a painful loss and couples can spend years and years working through this disappointment towards a more realistic view of what their relationship can offer. It will certainly be less romantic but for many couples this phase also heralds a greater intimacy because it's more truthful, and intimacy and closeness are always enhanced by feeling understood.

I wasn't sure whether Jack and Jill would take up the offer of couple psychotherapy, I thought that it might be too much for them – it seemed that they had built a life to protect them from disagreement and the rough and tumble of relationships. But, to my surprise, after some days of consideration, they wrote to say they'd like to come on a weekly basis to see me. They made it clear that this would be a big commitment; the journey would take them nearly two hours each way and so I, still in post-graduate training, felt some trepidation about whether their commitment would be matched by my capacity to help. It felt unnerving to work with a couple who were old enough to be my parents.

The next session didn't bring any further clarification of the problems between them, rather, they spoke obsessively about their neighbours and their fears about the council. They talked at length about their worry that they'd have to knock down the studio and how this would interfere with

Jack's preparation for the prestigious solo show he was going to have the following year. I heard endlessly about how important this was: his first solo exhibition and an honour. Something no gallery had ever offered him before.

'And how's that for you, Jill?' I asked. 'Perhaps it's quite a challenge for Jack to be doing this solo, without you?'

'The issue is the kiln,' she said, ignoring my question. 'It cost thousands and took weeks to put in and we simply can't afford to do that again. It took up the last of the money. If they say we have to demolish the studio, well, it's going to be . . .' she trailed off, her forehead furrowed like the twisted paper tissue in her hand. I began to feel that they were both terrified of talking about anything intimate. Was their fear of the studio being demolished also a metaphor for what they feared therapy might do to their relationship? But it was much too early to say this; they wouldn't hear it and wouldn't understand.

When they finally left, I made straight for my desk drawer and the packet of Silk Cut I kept there. Hauling myself onto the window ledge and cracking open the window, I perched on the stone windowsill and lit up. This was going to be a slow burn, I thought to myself.

Every one of us has a kind of internal template that shapes how we respond to others. As infants and children, we observe and absorb the relationships around us and these observations form interior images that shape our expectations and fears about intimacy. The impressions aren't fixed; I imagine them like a veil falling gently over our eyes, distorting reality, softening edges and giving us glimpses beyond. I think this is true for all of us but if our childhood experiences of family life have been fragile, destructive and frightening then the internal images we've formed of relationships can be very alarming, leaving us fearful and distrusting. Humans are vulnerable and fragile, easily wounded and easily hurt. More vulnerable than the animals closest to us, dogs, who seem to heal much more quickly than humans.

I was reminded of this when Mazy arrived during lockdown. A chunky mutt around a year old, she'd been patiently waiting in kennels in Bosnia, a street dog looking for a home. After three days' travelling in a lorry, locked in a crate, she was friendly but smelly when she met us. Mazy would take whatever was going, would wag her tail, but she wouldn't look you in the eye and would just as happily head off with the nearest stranger who looked like they had better treats. If we accidentally dropped the lead, she would run, oblivious to us, looking for her next meal ticket. Next came a period of rebellion and refusal to co-operate – a kind of selfish entitlement that meant treats were snatched and toys were guarded. Then, three months after her arrival, in early August, she seemed to relax and became more biddable. And then we fell in love. She'd look me deep in the eyes and I'd look back and that intense sense of connection was suddenly there. I trusted her and she trusted me. It amazed me. Mazy amazed me. I thought of all the years I'd worked with some of my patients and how slowly and painfully their trust had emerged. Dogs, it seems to me, are less fragile than humans. When hurt they can mend, and they can mend faster.

Jack and Jill hadn't mended. Whatever had troubled them in their childhood was now steering their current relationship. Something had scared them when they were little and their strategy to deal with the fear that they might get hurt again was to create a kind of shared idealised retreat, away from the world and from the ghosts that lived in the nursery.

The following week, I waited for Jack and Jill in my office. I had rung down to reception ten minutes earlier and been told they were on their way up. But where were they? My mind drifted back to the first session and how they'd 'disappeared' then too. I picked up the phone and rang down again, asking the receptionist to double-check they weren't still waiting to be invited up. But no, she told me, they'd already headed up.

Finally, I heard a quiet rustling outside my open door and, holding it wide, I could see Jack and Jill standing, as if in a queue, along the wall of the corridor. I gestured them in and slowly they made their way to the two chairs, which they perched gingerly on the edge of.

'Seems like you're feeling a bit hesitant about being here today,' I said, smiling warmly.

Jill stared at me and in her stare, I felt a huge yearning. But she said nothing and neither did Jack.

'I think you'd probably both like me to understand everything about you and your troubles without having to explain anything.'

Jack nodded and smiled.

'Perhaps that's what it's like between the two of you too? A feeling of needing to be understood without having to speak?'

Jack nodded again and Jill said, 'Yes, but . . .' She paused. 'But Jack doesn't seem to understand me now.'

I waited, hoping she would say more but she didn't.

'What is it, Jill, that he doesn't understand?' I asked. I knew this was a risky strategy, that asking a question might lead to me asking another, until I was essentially cross-examining her. But I felt I had to help her along a bit if we were to make any progress.

'I have no more income; we have no more money.'

I looked at Jack but his face was blank.

'That must be really quite frightening.'

Jill then began to speak, telling me she'd inherited money, a great deal of money. They'd lived off her inheritance since they left art school but the last of it had gone on building the studio. Jack needed it and so they built it but now they had nothing left. She shrugged her shoulders helplessly and again I looked at Jack who was staring out of the window.

I confess a wave of rage came over me. For God's sake Jack, I thought, get a grip. Then I wondered if this feeling in me was possibly linked to Jill's suppressed anger?

'Would you like Jack to be more engaged with this, Jill? Perhaps it feels like you're alone with the worry about money?'

She looked thoughtful and said, with an air of finality, 'I don't want to worry Jack.'

A sense of hopelessness came over me. Then I rallied and said, 'Do you feel concerned, Jack? About the financial situation?'

He shook his head and pursed his lips but didn't speak. I decided to be blunter.

'What would it mean for you, Jack, if the money runs out?'

He looked taken aback, as though this was a question he'd never considered. I could see that Jill was watching him intently. 'I don't really know. I think we'd be fine.'

The three of us sat in silence for some time. I felt hopeless and began to worry that they wouldn't come back and my training supervisor, whom I had to present the case to, would see me as a failure. I had to do something. But what?

The silence seemed interminable. Eventually, I said, 'I think in different ways you're both telling me how challenging it is to be here and how scary it is to discuss anything difficult between you. I noticed today that it took you a long time to come upstairs, as if you're both very reluctant in some way to start this process, and I notice that both of you seem very committed to keeping things smooth between you.'

Relief washed over me as Jack began to speak. 'Jill doesn't

seem to want to be . . . close. I don't know why and it's a bit of a shame . . .'

'Close?' I repeated.

'Yep. That's right. Close,' Jack said, looking down at his feet.

'Do you perhaps mean that you don't have any sexual intimacy anymore?'

They both nodded.

'Can you tell me a little about how that part of your life has been over the years?' I suggested.

Jack then spoke at some length about how they'd had a good sex life. How they were both virgins when they met and how, in those days, people didn't have sex before marriage. But they had and it was part of breaking free from their families. But then it stopped. They didn't seem to know why it had stopped and when I asked how long it was since they'd last had sex, I was shocked to hear that it was 25 years.

'I think it's less than that, Jack. Much less,' Jill said. Jack didn't look at her nor demur but simply sat stony-faced, looking at me.

I felt ill-equipped to respond. What could I usefully say to this couple who were nearly 30 years older than me?

The sessions continued like this for many weeks. Neither of them would speak without being prompted and my attempts to open up any exploration between them was met with silence, laughter or they changed the subject. It was my first salutary lesson in seeing how rigid and complete a couple's defences could be. They worked together seamlessly to keep me out. And yet, and yet, they kept coming, so I felt somewhere there was a part of them that hoped for change.

In the weekly case discussion group I attended as part of my training, Jack and Jill became a regular feature. I'd talk about them often, seeking help. My young colleagues would look sympathetically at me as I began to speak about the frustration I felt with the couple. My supervisor encouraged me to keep going, saying that by bearing the frustration and interpreting their fear of change, he believed that, sooner or later, like warm water on a lump of ice, they'd begin to melt and open things up.

Whilst the physical vista of my consulting room is simply its four white walls, each patient brings in, along with their problems, the richness of their internal and, indeed, their external life. They talk about their homes, their new sofa and the friends they've invited for lunch. They discuss holidays and argue over school choices, evoking in my mind's eye a home, a restaurant, a friend or even a meal. I follow my patients through their lives and on that journey, I try to help them make sense of all the feelings and conflicts that life provokes. However, just occasionally a patient brings nothing. No images. No events. No friends. The world they evoke inside me is empty, devoid of life. These are the most worrying cases and the hardest to bear.

Jack and Jill were like this. I had no images, no scenes or interactions inside my mind to help me understand their lives. All I had was their blankness, which seemed, despite their profession, to lack any colour or creativity. Issues they touched on, such as the lack of sex or money, though obviously important, somehow got dropped. Nothing seemed to get developed or resolved and I felt dull and frustrated, disappointed that nothing seemed to change or move. I was stuck. They were stuck.

Though I had enquired on several occasions, they'd told me very little about their early family lives and strangely, what they'd told me was so bland it seemed to slip from my mind as soon as they spoke. So I felt excited and alert when, during one session six months after they'd started therapy, Jill began to speak about her sister.

'She's coming to stay with us next week,' Jill said brightly. 'My younger sister, Joan. She's coming out of hospital.'

I waited and hoped my face showed that I was interested to hear more. I was now wary of becoming like a cross-examiner, asking question after question.

'She's schizophrenic. I think I told you.' I was sure she hadn't. 'She's coming to stay so I've been sorting out a room.' She paused. 'Which is difficult because it means moving so much stuff. I asked Jack to help but you're too busy, aren't you, Jack?'

Jack nodded. 'I'm not looking forward to this.'

'Her coming?' I queried. As usual, it was like getting blood out of a stone but gradually Jack admitted he was worried about Jill getting too tired, which would disrupt their work.

'Joan can be quite demanding, particularly of Jill. How are you going to get it all done if you've got to look after her all the time? We really need to focus on the show,' Jack said, his tone now slightly querulous.

'She's had it awfully hard, Jack. We've been lucky. She's been in and out of hospital all her life. I think she was very affected by what happened with my parents,' Jill said, addressing me.

'What happened with your parents?' I asked, suddenly curious and hoping that something important might now be shared. But I tried to hold my curiosity in check, if Jill could see how interested I was, she would shut down and disappear. It was like tempting a nervous wild animal to come and eat from your hand.

'Well. Long story,' she giggled awkwardly. And then she told me that her mother had often been ill with 'nervous complaints', which her father had found infuriating. There would be horrible fights where he would become violent, telling the children he was teaching their mother to behave.

It was painful to listen to and I began to feel sad for her.

'It must have been very frightening for you and your sister,' I said. But she didn't reply and, as Jill spoke more about her mother's illness, I began to wonder how much she'd had to disconnect from these traumatic events, losing the capacity to be in touch with many kinds of feelings.

'The problem was that even though my father would try quite patiently to explain to her that she couldn't spend all night locking and unlocking the doors, she just couldn't help herself. And then he'd explode and hit her.' Jill looked stricken and almost puzzled as she spoke.

As she continued, it began to be clear that her mother had suffered from obsessional compulsions. Jill described how she'd clean manically, even though they had maids. Her mother was terrified that she and her sister had lice in their hair and would insist on washing and combing their hair four or five times a day. When things were bad, her mother would lock herself in her bedroom and refuse to come out and sometimes that went on for days, perhaps weeks. Jill couldn't remember which.

'I think it was hard on Joan, she was so little. And in a different way for my elder brother, Ted.'

'Why for Ted?' I asked.

'He'd get involved. I'd run away and hide in the summer house, but Ted ...' She paused and looked at Jack. 'Ted would try to protect Mother. He'd always try to protect her and then my father would hit him too.'

She stopped and looked at me, then sighed but she didn't cry.

'He killed himself, you know. When he was 21. Just before I met you, wasn't it?' she said, turning to Jack.

He nodded but said nothing.

'Have you heard Jill talk about all this before, Jack?' I asked.

He shook his head, looking suddenly overwhelmed. 'I knew about Ted but not about the other stuff, no. I knew Jill's father was cranky and I knew your mother wasn't always well. But you never told me about this.' I thought how sad it was that Jill had never shared this with Jack, but I was beginning to understand how little they really talked about anything painful or difficult.

'Jack never met my mother; she died just before we graduated. Had a heart attack,' Jill said baldly.

'She was very thin,' Jack added.

'She didn't eat. She never ate. Neither did Ted.' And suddenly I noticed how thin Jack was. He looked half-starved.

After they left, I thought about what I'd been missing; everything seemed much more serious. I was suddenly aware of how vulnerable they were and that if Jack and Jill began to open things up, their stuck sameness might become something quite unstable and even, perhaps, perilous.

Something shifted in me after that. I stopped feeling frustrated and began to feel deep concern and, perhaps because they sensed my concern, they began to talk more freely in their sessions. I learnt that Joan had also tried to kill herself on several occasions. I learnt that before he died, Jill's father had developed Lewy Body Dementia, with the result he'd begun to have vivid, psychotic hallucinations. The doctors missed the dementia and he'd been committed to a psychiatric hospital; the same hospital that her mother had been in and out of. The more I learnt about her family, the more I began to understand just why she'd retreated 'into the woods' with Jack.

As the weeks passed, it became clear that Joan was causing problems between them. She demanded lots of care and attention, which disrupted the seemingly smooth, unruffled surface of their life. Where once they talked haltingly about the neighbours and the planning department, they now talked incessantly about Joan. I heard about the mess she'd left in the kitchen, about her wandering about at night, leaving on all the lights, and I had the sense, and said so, that whilst this was a nuisance, it was also a way for them to bond with each other. The problems, once again, were outside of their relationship – they could cosily join up against a common enemy, such as the planners or now, it seemed, Joan.

However, one small but significant difference between them began to be tentatively expressed. For some time, they'd been talking about how much time it was taking for Jack to make this one piece. The sculpture seemed to involve a complex mosaic of thousands of glass shards and Jack was increasingly stressed that it would never be completed on time. After hearing about this problem for the fifth time, I found myself asking if they'd ever thought about getting any help? I knew many artists had studio assistants.

'We never allow anyone but us into the studio,' Jack insisted.

I thought about how the studio seemed like a kind of microcosm of their relationship, something that shut out the world – a kind of retreat.

'Why not?' I asked. I was feeling that they needed a challenge. Their complete agreement over Joan's misdeeds had left me wanting to disrupt their accord.

'Well, we just never do. No one would be able to help; it's not like that, Susanna,' Jack blustered.

'Maybe Joan could help. She could polish the glass. She could even stick the glass,' Jill said tentatively.

'I don't think so. She wouldn't anyway,' Jack said, dismissing her. Turning to me, he added, 'She's very lazy. She doesn't get out of bed till midday.' He laughed.

'I don't know. It could be good for her. And it'd really help me,' Jill uncharacteristically persisted.

Jack shrugged and then they began to talk about Joan's slovenly ways again, smoothing down the little ripple that had emerged between them.

But these differences began to emerge more frequently. I could see that Jill was beginning to find her own voice, challenging Jack just a little. Had it helped her to watch me gently challenge him? Was she beginning to feel less frightened of taking her own view?

It was September and I'd been working with Jack and Jill for nearly a year. I'd just returned from my summer break and it was the first session back. As usual, I phoned down to reception to tell them to come up and, once again, the minutes ticked past the hour and they didn't appear. I stood in the doorway looking down the long corridor towards the lifts expecting them at any minute to emerge. The lift doors opened and a group of people tumbled out but Jack and Jill were not amongst them. I went back into my office and dialled down to reception but, though I tried several times, the phone was engaged and I couldn't get through. I looked anxiously down the corridor again – still no sign. Where were they?

It was nearly twenty past the hour when I heard their footsteps outside my door, I jumped up from my chair and held the door wide as they shuffled in. I waited patiently, though I didn't feel patient, as they arranged their bags and then we sat down, looking at each other intently.

'Was there a problem downstairs?' I asked. 'I wondered where you'd got to.'

They looked embarrassed; Jill had her head lowered and Jack avoided my eye. A kind of awkwardness descended on the room and I felt myself grow hot with discomfort, though I didn't understand why. Had I asked something I shouldn't?

Jill raised her head. 'I'm sorry we kept you waiting.

Sometimes, we go in the toilets . . . together . . . for a cuddle. Sometimes, and I think it's when we're stressed out, we have a cuddle in the toilets before coming in.' And then she looked at Jack and they both laughed and so did I as I remembered all the other times they'd seemed to take forever coming up from the waiting room. 'Maybe some of the stress today is coming back after the long break?' I said.

It was quiet then for a while and then Jill spoke again. 'Joan's back in hospital. I took her back last weekend.' She looked glum. 'She smashed up one of Jack's pieces in the studio.'

I drew a sharp, shocked intake of breath and looked at Jack who sighed mightily as he slowly began to speak. 'Yup, completely destroyed it. With a hammer.'

There was something shocking about this destruction, such a counterpoint to Jack and Jill's impassive calm. 'Mad' Joan, amok with a hammer, whilst they sat there and calmly explained that the piece wasn't in fact one that Jack planned to show and what a relief it had been that she hadn't smashed 'Cave'.

'Cave?' I questioned.

'Oh, that's the piece Joan was helping with and it's really large and an important piece. That would've been a complete disaster if she'd taken a hammer to that!'

They began to talk about the piece – how intricate it was and how they hoped it would sell. The piece appeared to be a kind of inverted mosaic, most of which was hidden from view. They talked on and on about the number of glass pieces that were involved and how much Jack's dealer thought it might sell for. At first, I felt quite engaged with their chatter but then I remembered Joan and this shocking act of violence.

'As you talk about this piece of sculpture, it makes me think how much *you* both hide from view; how much you both retreat into a kind of cave, away from painful things.

You've told me that something terrible and violent has happened, yet it's very difficult for you to really stay with that. Perhaps, also, the thought of talking to me about this made you retreat together into a kind of "toilet cave" before the session?'

Jack looked at me glaringly, clearly annoyed.

'I don't know why we come to see you, Susanna. I really didn't *want* to come today. I don't see the point and if Jill wasn't so *into* it, I'm afraid I'd never come again. I really don't think it's useful to dig all of this up; we need to look forward, not back. I've got to focus on the exhibition now, not Joan or this . . . stuff.'

I'd never heard Jack be so tetchy or so forthcoming and it felt like a huge relief that here he was, for the first time, speaking his mind.

'Don't be so rude, Jack!' Jill interjected. 'Susanna's just trying to help us. I'm sick of you being so negative about our sessions.'

'I don't think it *is* helpful. If Susanna hadn't suggested it, Joan wouldn't have come into the studio at all. And the whole thing's really upset everything and put it all back. And you've been in a complete state since. How is that helpful?' Jack concluded, his face reddened and his voice shaky with rage.

It was as though some dam had broken and something raw and violent was now exposed in him. The anger so long suppressed now sat in the room. I tried to speak about how frightening these feelings were and how much they'd tried to avoid them but I didn't get very far. The session ended badly, with neither of them looking me in the eye as they left.

I was concerned but unsurprised when the following week I got a message from them saying they were sorry but they couldn't come today. They'd never cancelled a session before and I felt worried that they'd been so frightened by the conflict that they'd now terminate the therapy. I sat in the consulting room alone, chewing on my biro as I drafted a letter to say that I looked forward to seeing them next week. But the following week, I waited for the hour and, again, they didn't come. I checked with the office. Had they called? No, they hadn't. I drafted another letter acknowledging how difficult the last session had been and reminding them that I'd be waiting for them the following week. I knew if they didn't arrive again, I'd probably have to close the case and that would cause problems with my training and leave me feeling I'd failed and let Jack and Jill down. My group of fellow trainees consoled me and my supervisor talked about how couples could powerfully avoid change if it threatened their relationship.

By the following week, I expected nothing; they hadn't been in touch, and I was sure they weren't going to come. So it was much to my surprise when at 3pm on the dot the phone rang and the receptionist informed me that Jack and Jill were on their way up. Seconds later, I heard them coming along the corridor and I opened the door to let them in.

'We're really sorry about last week, Susanna,' Jill said hurriedly as she sat down. 'We should have been in touch but we've had such a difficult time.' She nodded her head at Jack and I followed her gaze to Jack's hand, which was hidden under a substantial bandage.

Jack looked at me and there was something shamefaced and awkward in his gaze.

'What happened?' I asked gently.

'You say,' Jack appealed to Jill. I looked at Jill, who looked shrunken and old, as though all the life had been sucked out of her.

'He stabbed himself with a point chisel. He had an . . . an . . . upset and afterwards he went into the studio and, well, er . . . hurt himself.'

There was a silence.

'He was in hospital. Just got out yesterday . . .' she said, trailing off, her voice barely audible.

It took some time but gradually I heard how they had had to call an ambulance and how, in casualty, Jack had become so distressed that they'd admitted him to the psychiatric ward. I said how frightening this must have been, for Jack himself and for Jill to see Jack like this, when he was always so quiet and controlled.

They reacted to my comments with silence. Jack, head bowed, stared at his hand and Jill looked at him expectantly.

'It's not the first time, Susanna. I've seen him like this before. He's done it before,' Jill said awkwardly, as though confessing something to me that was secret.

I turned to Jack. Would he say more?

'When we were students. I got in a state just before our finals, our graduation show.'

'You cut your wrists,' Jill interjected, challenging Jack to be more specific.

'Yep,' Jack nodded reluctantly. 'Yes, I did. I thought I was going to fail.'

The atmosphere in the room felt electric, as though Jill was humiliating him and stripping Jack of every ounce of his pride. I could feel the sense of shame and sadness that sat between them and I felt I had to find a way to help Jack speak about himself.

But it wasn't Jack who spoke then; it was Jill who told me about the psychiatrist they'd talked to and the discussion of medication and the follow-up appointment they had to attend next week. And, as she talked, I felt her soothing Jack. She talked almost as if it was she who had stabbed herself, as though it was both of them who were due to see the doctor next Tuesday. I felt wrapped up in this comforting chatter whilst Jack stayed silent, imprisoned in his feelings. The moment of raw honesty had evaporated and we were back to everything being shut down between them. Every feeling was to be calmed and everything I said or tried to explore as the session went on was met with resistance and smiles.

My mind drifted; I felt powerless to help them be more real. Perhaps I was even wrong to try to open this up – after all, stirring things up seemed to have made things worse. Maybe they just needed to settle things down and go back to what they felt safe with. Who was I to know?

I sat there, gloomy and uncertain how to help, so I said nothing and we sat in silence as Jill's mollifying chatter trailed off.

'Maybe, we've been wondering, should we perhaps take a bit of a break from seeing you?' Jill began again. 'I think we'll be seeing the psychiatrist for a while . . . maybe it would be better if we just did that?'

'Perhaps you're worried it'll be too much for Jack? You want to protect him and think maybe it'd be easier for him to stop coming here?'

'Yes, I think so.'

We both looked at Jack, waiting for his input.

'We'll keep coming. You want to come, Jill, so we'll keep coming,' Jack said.

'It's fine, Jack. We can come back when you're feeling better,' Jill responded. 'We could come back, couldn't we?' Jill asked, looking anxiously at me.

Jill's anxious fussing felt stultifying and I had a sense this over-protectiveness would force Jack into further silence. And then suddenly I thought about Jill's brother and his suicide. Was this what made Jill so careful not to upset Jack? Was she like this because she was always terrified that *he'd* kill himself?

'I was thinking, Jill, about your brother and how you said how much Jack, when you first met, had reminded you of him.'

She nodded and I went on.

'And I was noticing right now how much you seem to want to protect Jack, even when I can see you've got quite a lot of your own feelings about what's happened.'

She nodded again, though less emphatically.

'I suppose I was thinking that this wish to protect Jack might be so strong because you're very worried that history might repeat itself and you might lose Jack the same way you lost your brother.'

'Is that right?' Jack asked, looking intently at Jill. 'Is that what you're worried about?'

Jill gave a little shrug. 'Maybe . . . maybe.' She mused. And then she talked more about Ted and how much she missed him. His death had come completely out of the blue and to this day she didn't understand why he'd killed himself. She described how he took his life by driving his van off the cliffs near where they'd grown up. They'd all had lunch together the day before and he'd seemed fine, his usual self. Then we all sat in silence, thinking about Ted as Jill quietly wept.

'It seems you've never really been able to make sense of your brother's death. Do you feel you can understand why Jack tried to hurt himself?' I asked.

'Not really, no. I know I should but I don't. I don't.'

'Perhaps it feels very dangerous to ask him, Jill?'

She nodded and looked at Jack expectantly but he was silent, wrapped in his own terror.

'I don't know *what* he's thinking, Susanna. I used to. But now, I don't think I do.'

'Maybe that sense that you really knew each other's thoughts, felt so close and sure of each other has changed?'

'Jill's changed,' Jack said baldly.

'Have I? I haven't! I don't think I have. Have I?'

'In what way has Jill changed, Jack?' I asked.

'Do you still love me?' Jack said, ignoring me now as he turned to Jill.

'Of course I do. I do! Is that why you stabbed yourself? Is it? I do love you Jack, I do. Oh, I do.'

Back then, I felt disappointed that I didn't help Jack and Jill more. I had the zeal and idealism of a young therapist and didn't understand that a couple only need change a very little bit to make life more rewarding and hopeful. They had been a 'babes in the wood' couple and their whole relationship was structured to keep out the dark and scary uncertainties that had threatened them in their childhoods. Gradually they'd come a little way out of this retreat and faced the things in themselves and each other that had haunted them for years. They'd become more open and authentic with each other, and even with me, and, like with all relationships, this openness brought a greater resilience to themselves and their marriage.

Jack began to see a psychoanalyst on his own, which not only helped him with his fears but made Jill feel a bit less responsible for him and for always making sure he was OK. Eventually, after four years, I was leaving the clinic and we agreed that this seemed like it was the right time to stop the couple therapy. I think we could have gone on forever. There was something timeless about the way they lived their lives and that timelessness got into the work with me. We'd become comfortable together and, though from time to time they'd show me that they could be different people with different minds, their longing to be as one was deep inside them. I think they just felt safest there.

KRISTOF KEEPS KISSING THE FROG

I sometimes wonder if humans are up to managing all the feelings that our biology seems to have endowed us with. Years ago, I used to have a recurring dream that I was driving a car but I was too small to reach the pedals with my feet. The car careered towards disaster as I strained to touch the brake. Did the dream represent my anxiety that I wouldn't be able to manage my own feelings? A childhood hangover, perhaps, of those early experiences of being a toddler, overwhelmed by emotions and unable to contain them? As we grow older, most of us learn not to stamp our feet and roll about on the floor wailing but love affairs can still evoke emotions that spin our heads.

For some patients, it can come as a shock to discover that they have feelings and wishes they have no conscious awareness of. Because feelings can be so powerful, humans find all sorts of ways of repressing them. Some people sublimate their desires in physical activity. Others use an intense focus on work, a video game or a gripping novel. Sometimes we can somatise repressed emotions, so they get expressed by our body in the form of a headache, a backache or a mysterious stomach upset. And there are, of course, less healthy avenues we adopt to repress and manage emotions, where we numb ourselves with alcohol or drugs.

But there is one form of managing feelings that is far less known and generally understood, which in psychoanalytic theory is known as 'projection'. Projection is a mental process whereby we attribute to someone else something we reject or disown in ourselves. A typical and common example, which most of us will have employed at some time or another, is when we feel ashamed about a feeling, such as being greedy or aggressive, and shed that shame by identifying that trait in others.

Projection can also help explain the inexplicable, such as how and why humans can descend into mass hatred of others and genocide. We have unfortunately seen many situations where one group demonises another group as having ugly traits, such as dishonesty or greed, and then attacks them in a hateful and sometimes murderous way for these traits. One group is then 'pure' whilst the other is filled up with all these reviled qualities.

In a less dramatic way, projection is something I frequently see in the consultancy room. One patient, who came to see me because he was struggling with lethargy and depression, began a session by telling me that over the weekend he'd taken his teenage son to task for spending all weekend playing video games and staring into his phone. The patient complained that he'd bought his son a guitar *and* paid for lessons, but he never practised or buckled down to learning or doing anything useful. It didn't take long for us to understand that he was shouting at his son for exactly the things he felt most anxious about in himself, which was his *own* difficulty with being productive and proactive. He'd started therapy because he felt a failure and had, over his lifetime, been unable to fulfil his promise. Together, we came to understand that he'd been distancing himself from these feelings by accusing his boy of being lazy and aimless. As this realisation dawned on him, his frustration with his son lessened and their relationship improved.

There is also a more specific kind of projection that commonly occurs between intimate partners called 'projective identification'. This process occurs when we project a trait we don't like in ourselves onto our partner and they, often wordlessly and without even realising it, take it off us. If, for example, we've grown up in a family where vulnerability is perceived as shameful and 'weak', we may shed that shame by projecting our vulnerability into our partner and then we treat them as if they are very fragile. The wonderful thing is that if our partner isn't too bothered or ashamed of their vulnerability (maybe they grew up in a family where it was OK to feel a bit needy at times) we can find ourselves, gradually over time, less worried about being 'weak'. We've learnt something emotionally from our partner – that the trait we felt ashamed about isn't actually as bad as we thought. In this way, we can begin to know and like parts of ourselves that we've previously denied. And of course, this spurs psychological growth and development. This is the wonderfully creative part of relationships, where we learn and mature emotionally within a loving partnership.

Sometimes the projected trait is 'held' by one partner for years and years. An example is where one person (often the woman) feels anxiety, whilst the other (often the man) simply doesn't. Perhaps women are more comfortable with the feeling of being anxious whereas men prefer a self-image that's unruffled, stoic and calm? The woman frets about the children, the damp patch in the bedroom and her mother's health, whilst the man remains apparently unbothered. Partners often divide up feelings in this way so that one person holds a difficult feeling on behalf of the couple. However, my years as a couple therapist have taught me that often, despite appearances to the contrary, the biggest anxieties, which appear to be felt by only one partner, are actually shared.

*

Julian and Kristof had been together more than ten years. They seemed charming on first meeting and told me they needed help because they couldn't agree whether they should become parents.

Kristof dressed beautifully in clothes that were just on the edge of looking too young for him. He was in his forties and looked very fit but he had a worn look and his skin was lined as though he'd had too much sun. Every so often, he'd smile or laugh, his face would light up and he'd suddenly look like a little boy. This boyish quality created a maternal feeling in me that suggested he needed a lot of love and care.

Julian, despite being eight years younger than Kristof, was much more sober and restrained, his face unlined and unmoving. He always wore a navy suit and polished brogues to the sessions and rarely spoke without being asked a question.

In early sessions, they established what appeared to be the nub of their problem, which was that all the feelings and longing belonged to Kristof. He was the one who wanted them to have children; the one who wanted more sex; the one who wanted a holiday and the one who wanted a new sofa. Whatever they discussed, whether it was becoming parents or moving to a new house, Kristof took the lead and Julian either complied or passively resisted. It was as if Julian had no wishes and no desires of his own and was working as hard as he could to be invisible.

This was very frustrating to work with. When I offered Kristof my thoughts and understanding about what was happening between them, he'd listen eagerly, seeming to absorb it. Or, at other times, he'd reshape my thought and make it his own, and though this could be because he'd initially disagreed with my idea, it was quite often to begin a playful and creative exchange. In short, he appeared to be letting me help him.

Julian responded quite differently. When I offered him some understanding that I hoped would reach his heart, he seemed to let it roll down from his chest and off his body. He didn't so much reject my thoughts – he simply didn't engage with them. It was exasperating. I tried and tried to get closer to Julian but it felt as though he was impervious. Although he was always polite and listened earnestly, it seemed as though he simply didn't have any emotional insight or opinions about their issues. Kristof owned them all. Julian would say he was fine, everything was fine, and it seemed this couple mutually accepted that Kristof was the one who was upset, anxious and needy. Often, I'd spend an entire session listening to Kristof complaining and appealing to Julian in a rather desperate way, whilst Julian, though not overtly aggressive, sat silent, pretty much unmoved.

Experience had taught me that this situation, which seemed so polarised, was almost certainly a shared problem. What could be the underlying reason why they'd shaped their relationship in this way? For a long time, I simply couldn't understand what was holding them together so powerfully. I was, however, interested in the fact that Julian, who was seemingly so compliant and yet so empty in the sessions, was by far the most successful at work. He had set up a tech business in his twenties and now employed close to 100 people. It was challenging to imagine how this man, who sat so colourlessly on my grey couch, had the gumption and drive to create such a successful business. I began to notice that whenever (though it was very occasionally) we talked about his work, he'd become much more animated. I commented on more than one occasion that all Julian's passion and ambition seemed to be lodged in his work, whilst Kristof held the passion and ambition for the relationship.

Interestingly, when Julian talked about his work, Kristof would grow sulkily silent. But then the conversation would take its usual turn and flow back to Kristof's sense of deprivation and longing. Nothing seemed to be changing, which, of course, started to leave me as frustrated as Kristof.

The question of 'progress' in treatment is a complicated one in psychoanalytic therapy. In cognitive behaviour therapy (CBT), the aim is usually what we would call 'symptom reduction'. For instance, if a patient comes with depression, once that depression has lifted, the treatment is complete. In other therapies, 'goals' for treatment are discussed and agreed between patient and therapist and a set number of sessions are arranged to try to meet them. Psychoanalytic treatment isn't like that at all, which is why some people are critical of it. But the exciting thing about working in this way is the experience of something unfolding, of great new connections being made, of the yawning canyon between feeling and understanding being occasionally bridged. And when feeling and thinking come together, it can really help us stand in our own shoes and have the sensation of being whole. Many people who come to see me are really quite frightened, though they won't necessarily consciously know it. Understanding what frightens them, looking it in the eye and recognising the origins of that fear, is life affirming and life expanding. It brings us closer to our own emotional truth and this promotes mental growth.

But couple therapy is somewhat different to individual psychoanalytic treatment because couples often come with a more specific agenda. They want to stop arguing; they want to have sex; they want to agree on where to live or how to discipline their children. They come because they hope by coming, they'll feel happier or more content. Or they come because they're in two minds as to whether to stay together or separate. They may learn a huge amount about themselves (sometimes a great deal more than in an individual therapy) but they usually still want to resolve

something and then end their therapy, shutting their bedroom door behind them.

And what do I want as a therapist? I've been trained not
to want very much at all. The influential British psychoanalyst
Wilfred Bion cautioned the psychoanalyst against 'desire'.
The job of the analyst is not to want a particular outcome for
a patient or even for a session. The job of the analyst, he said,
was simply to be truly present with the patient without a
whole set of pre-conceived thoughts or expectations. To
uncover the truth of a person, the psychoanalyst must be
wholly available, without all the baggage of previous experience or knowledge. 'The psychoanalyst should aim at
achieving a state of mind so that at every session he feels he
has not seen the patient before.'*

This way of thinking has helped me (an impatient person) to be more patient. I'm also quite clear that my patient's
development will take its own time and, though I foster this
emotional growth by my presence, interest and curiosity, I
can't force it to happen.

Nevertheless, despite this training, I confess I was very
exasperated by this case. I found Kristof easier than Julian but
as the months went on and his continual complaints didn't
change, I found myself becoming frustrated with him too.

We were 14 months into their therapy when something happened. Julian and Kristof's regular weekly session time was
late on a Thursday evening. They were usually my last patients
of the week, which of course didn't make my frustration any
easier to bear. But one Tuesday evening at 6.30, I was just
packing up for the day when my buzzer went, which was curious as I wasn't expecting anyone.

* Wilfred Bion, 'Notes on Memory and Desire', first published in *The
Psychoanalytic Forum*, vol. 2, no. 3 (1967).

I lifted the receiver to hear the cheery voice of Kristof saying, as he usually did, 'Hi, it's Kristof, we're heeere!'

For a moment, I felt utterly confused. What day was it? What time? And, indeed, I said this aloud down the receiver. I could hear an intake of breath at the end of the line and then Kristof's voice saying to Julian, 'We've got the wrong day.'

'Oh dear. Yes, I think you have,' I replied.

We quickly ended this strange conversation over the intercom, with them laughing nervously and saying they'd see me on Thursday. I paused a little while in my consulting room to give them time to get on their way, then left for home, pondering on this turn of events.

Two days later, on Thursday, I waited with some anticipation for Julian and Kristof to arrive. I imagined that Julian would be ashamed of the mistake but I doubted he would show it, whilst Kristof would extravagantly express his 'mortification' at the incident.

They kept me waiting quite a while and it occurred to me that perhaps they weren't going to come. But then, 12 minutes late, the buzzer went and they entered my room in a rush.

'Oh, my goodness,' Kristof said breathlessly, 'what idiots were we!' And he proceeded to explain that Julian had texted him that afternoon to meet outside John Lewis, which was the usual place they met before walking together to my office. Kristof, who hadn't been working that day, left home, got on the Tube and met Julian without any thought that they'd got the wrong day. All of this was delivered with great hilarity and extravagant gestures. Gradually, however, as he continued to grandstand, he began to blame and shame Julian.

'Thing is . . . Julian can't wait to see you, Susanna. Every week, he asks me if we're seeing you on Thursday when he's already got it in his diary! I don't know why but he talks about you all the time! Don't you, dearest?' he said, smirking.

As you can imagine, I felt most surprised by this information. Julian, who sat so impassively every week, had given absolutely no indication at all of any devotion to the therapy and certainly not to me. Everything about him made me feel as though he came dutifully, not enthusiastically. I also wondered about Kristof exposing Julian in this way. It was rather cruel and made me wonder what feeling, at that moment, he was trying to get 'out' of him and 'into' Julian. Shame? Neediness? A feeling of humiliation?

I said, 'Perhaps you both feel a little ashamed about turning up two days early? Maybe it feels humiliating to make that kind of mistake? Maybe it makes you both feel it reveals your attachment to me and to coming here, leaving you rather vulnerable?'

They both looked serious and nodded and slowly they began to talk about how important the sessions were and how they looked forward to them.

'We wouldn't still be together if we weren't seeing you,' said Julian, before uncharacteristically adding, 'Kristof would have left me by now.'

There was a silence that yawned between them and Kristof, who looked confused and querulous, responded, 'I don't know why you think I would have left . . . much, much more likely that you would have.'

I was interested in this new development and how it now seemed clearer that they shared a fear that the other would end the relationship. Kristof had certainly expressed this concern before but not Julian. Was something shifting?

Some weeks went by and at each session they seemed to be becoming more open. Whereas before we seemed to go around the same issues over and over, new avenues of discussion were beginning to open up. Just before the Easter break, I started the session by reminding them I was going to be away for two weeks. They both looked subdued and nodded and Julian, in a businesslike manner, patted his phone and said, 'Yes, in the diary.' Then neither of them spoke for quite some time.

I said, 'Perhaps it feels quite upsetting to have a break from sessions at this time?'

Kristof ignored my comment and, addressing Julian, said, 'I think we need to talk to Susanna about what you said on Saturday.'

Julian squirmed uncomfortably and glared at Kristof. 'Be my guest,' he answered.

At this, Kristof began to recount their conversation. They'd talked seriously at the weekend about splitting up because Julian had decided he didn't want to progress any plans about having children. Ever. He didn't want things to change between them; he thought Kristof wouldn't be able to cope with a child's demands and he couldn't bear to go through the whole process of trying to find a surrogate or trying to adopt. He wasn't going to do it. Not now. Not ever. After a pause, Kristof concluded by saying, 'If children are off the table, then I told him we couldn't really go on. We just don't want the same things and don't have a future.'

A gloomy sense of doom settled into the room. Julian sat upright, staring into the distance, avoiding my eye and Kristof, his arms crossed, shoulders slumped, glanced back and forth between me and his partner.

For the rest of the session, I tried to get them to be more in touch with their sadness. I spoke about how desperate this situation felt to them and tried to explore their feelings about their seemingly unbridgeable differences but they didn't really respond and stayed in their angry bubbles. I felt alarmed. Were they going to split in this precipitous way? Suddenly their relationship, which had up till now felt so solidly stuck, seemed very precarious.

This uncertainty often goes along with change. Whilst some couples make steady progress and some couples make no progress at all, there is often a kind of jeopardy in the process of lasting change. This jeopardy can lead to a break-up or it can even lead to a breakdown; opening things up and getting in touch with feelings that have been long repressed can be perilous, requiring the therapist to 'hold' the patient carefully through this period of instability and transformation. Were Kristof and Julian about to break up or about to break through?

I said some general words about how one of the most corrosive things couples can do is make threats to end the relationship, how these threats heighten anxieties about abandonment and undermine basic security and trust. I wondered if they were really in touch with what a big step this was and suggested that we could talk more about this next week before they decided. They both agreed.

Three days later I got a text from Julian informing me Kristof had moved out and asking for a session as soon as possible. It seemed such a breakthrough for Julian to make this kind of request that I agreed to see him the following day. As he entered my room, I thought how shell-shocked he looked. He sat on the sofa, stiffly upright, his eyes wide and glassy, and robotically recounted the events leading up to Kristof leaving.

'Kristof's at Francine's, you know his sister . . .' he trailed off and we sat in silence. Eventually, I asked him to tell me more about what had happened after the last session and he painstakingly explained that Kristof had become angry with him and said that he now realised he'd been wasting his time. Julian shrugged at this and waited for me to ask more; he seemed unmoved, as usual, even though it seemed he'd just lost his partner.

'You're very certain about not wanting children?' I asked.

As usual, a question from me, made him squirm. 'I don't know. Not really, I just kinda feel it's not really going to happen. I think it's just too much of a long shot, really. I can't see us being able to go through with the whole thing. And, to be honest, I don't think Kristof could cope with it. I just don't think we're in a good enough place to do something like that. How can we be talking about splitting up and having children at the same time? It seems ridiculous to me.'

It occurred to me, as he fumbled for words, that these muddled feelings might be linked to them being a gay couple and I wondered if I could find a way to explore that with him.

'I wonder, Julian, whether you think that you and Kristof would make good parents?' I asked tentatively.

'Not sure we would, to be honest,' Julian replied.

'Why not?'

'Lots of things. Not sure either of us are . . . cut out for it.'

'Cut out for it? Because you're gay?'

Julian shrugged, looking uncertain how to respond. 'Maybe.'

'Perhaps a part of you doesn't think a gay couple could make a family? Be good parents?'

'My parents certainly wouldn't,' Julian responded, suddenly animated. 'They'd be . . . horrified.'

Julian then began to talk about his family and how much they'd disapprove. They could barely look him and Kristof in the eye and he couldn't imagine what they'd do if he had a kid.

'Kristof simply doesn't seem to understand my family. His sisters and his mother are just so different to mine, not . . .'

'Homophobic?' I supplied.

'Yes, I guess so,' Julian said in a flat voice. 'Kristof just doesn't get that things are complicated; he just wants what he wants and gets so upset when I can't always give it to him.'

'You're describing how angry and upset Kristof is but I'm noticing that *you* seem almost unmoved?' I commented. He looked at me long and hard, as though, like a child, he was trying to win a staring competition. 'I wonder what happens to your feelings, Julian? You seem not to feel any anger or sadness, despite Kristof leaving.'

At that point, he seemed to give up. He dropped his head and began to cry. I felt a surge of compassion – a feeling that Julian rarely generated in me – and I spoke to him about how hard he found it to let himself grieve. Abruptly, he stopped crying and said with bitterness and anger, 'What's the fucking point of crying? It won't bring him back.'

'It might,' I said. 'I think Kristof would be shocked to see you so distressed; I don't think you've ever shown these kinds of feelings to him, or me, before?'

He nodded and he began to talk tentatively about how he really did care hugely for Kristof but that he really hated feeling this way. He felt as though Kristof had trapped him into something and was always trying to trap him further.

'I wonder what you feel the trap is?' I said. 'Perhaps if you acknowledge that you want him and a life with him, you fear he'll drop you? If you can tell yourself that you don't really care about him, you can maintain an illusion you won't be hurt? I do wonder, Julian, what happened to you in childhood that has made it so hard for you to show you need people?'

I waited and watched Julian, hoping that now he'd open up more about his childhood. He'd told me so little and in such a factual way that I still had little real picture of his family. If things were to shift between him and Kristof, something needed to be unlocked. We would have to get closer to understanding why he feared showing his feelings and why connecting to his needs was so hard for him.

Julian looked thoughtful. 'You know I went to boarding school at seven?'

'At seven? No, I didn't know you went so young. I thought you went when you were older. Do you know why they sent you at such a young age?'

He shook his head. 'I don't remember but my mother, you know, wasn't very loving. She always says I was very clingy. I don't think she could stand it.'

I noticed he used the word 'it' but I wondered if he meant 'me'.

Julian told me he remembered his mother always promising to come up and kiss him goodnight if he put himself to bed. He'd sit on the landing waiting and waiting and then sometimes, when he couldn't wait any longer, he'd go downstairs to see her and then his father would laugh at him and take him back upstairs and spank him for getting out of bed.

I imagined him as a little boy, wanting his mother so badly. I felt my eyes welling up. How could his parents have neglected him so cruelly? How could his father have mocked him for wanting attention? But whilst I was full of feeling, Julian had recounted the story coldly, as if it concerned someone else.

'Julian, it seems you can't connect to that little boy you're describing. It's as though you've lost touch with some part of yourself, as though you're frozen. I think you avoid feeling things – to want, to desire, to need Kristof is just too dangerous. To have passionate, loving feelings for him is somehow . . . shameful.'

He then spoke of several humiliations during his childhood but perhaps the most telling was that whenever his father spanked him – which happened often – he would wet himself and his father would become even more furious, telling him he was pathetic and disgusting.

As the session went on, Julian began to connect his inability to declare his feelings for Kristof with these childhood experiences. He said one thing he knew was that he never wanted to depend on anyone.

Once Julian left, I composed an email to them both, saying that I was sorry things had become so difficult, letting Kristof know I'd seen Julian separately and encouraging them to come on Thursday. I felt bad that I'd failed to help them manage this crisis but it was possible that Julian and Kristof, who'd been stuck in the same gear for so long, were now beginning a process of great change. Whether this change would make or break their relationship, we just had to wait and see.

The rest of my week was busy. I was writing a book review and had a string of meetings on top of my usual practice. I thought about Julian and Kristof from time to time but when Thursday evening came around, it still wasn't certain they were coming. At 6.30pm I suddenly felt a wave of huge disappointment. Was the work going to end like this? I felt dumped and confused. Surely, this couple who'd seemed so attached to each other would try to work things out?

As the minutes dragged on, I began to lose hope. I looked at my phone – no message. I contemplated drafting an email and had just written '*Dear Julian and Kristof*,' when the buzzer went.

For the first time in their treatment, Julian, ashen but alert, entered the room first. Kristof, behind him, lacked his usual bounce, shuffling in rather reluctantly, eyes down as if he was entering the headteacher's office. Julian uncharacteristically started, apologising for being late and then launching into documenting recent developments.

'Well, I did what you told me. We saw each other last

night and I told Kristof how much I cared about him and how I wanted it to work, just like you said.'

It was impossible not to notice how Julian had failed to take ownership of his own desire to woo Kristof back but instead couched it in a way that suggested that, like a good little boy, he was simply following my orders. Having delivered his crisp report, Julian went silent, waiting, as usual, for someone else to take up the reins.

Kristof was unmoved and something in his presence seemed grumpy, so I commented on how he appeared reluctant to be here. He responded by admitting the only reason he'd come was because he knew how much I'd been trying to help them and didn't want to let me down.

The atmosphere felt hopeless and I felt myself sinking into my own thoughts as we all sat in a gloomy silence. After a while, I looked up and saw the stricken look on Julian's face; there were beads of sweat on his forehead and he was glancing anxiously at Kristof, who stared at the floor, his expression closed. I caught his eye but instead of responding to my look, he turned to Kristof.

'Please come home, Kristof. Why do you have to leave? Susanna doesn't think you have to.'

Kristof remained impassive and spoke with heavy sarcasm. 'Well let me list it for you. We're going to split up because you don't want children. You don't want sex. You don't want to move. You don't want to go on holiday and you never want to talk about anything!'

Julian started to well up. 'You seem so certain of that, Kristof,' I observed. 'And yet I think Julian was trying to tell you something different.'

Julian interrupted. 'It's not that I don't want those things. It's not that I don't love you. I do. It's just that I don't know whether we can manage the whole process . . . see it through . . . and that you won't end up leaving me anyway.'

Kristof shook his shoulders dismissively.

'I'm just not sure you won't leave,' Julian repeated. 'What if it doesn't go right? A baby is so demanding. I don't know that we've got that much, you know . . . energy.'

'What? What? I've got the energy. I'm always giving and look how patient I've been with you. Look how long I've coped with you and all your faffing about.'

'But I've just said how much I love you.'

'Because Susanna told you to.'

'No. I mean it. I'm just frightened whether we'd be able to see it through with a child. It's a huge responsibility. And financially that'll all be on me. And I'm frightened that I mightn't be able to look after a child like you want me to.' He paused. 'And that you might not be able to cope with the child's needs.'

I asked Julian whether this lack of confidence could be linked to the feelings he'd had as a small boy, when his mother couldn't bear his neediness. Could this, perhaps, be informing his worry that Kristof might not be able to bear a child's neediness?

There was silence. I didn't think Julian had taken in what I said but I thought Kristof had heard it. Julian put out his hand to Kristof in a simple gesture of hope. I looked at it suspended in mid-air, with its unspoken request that Kristof take it. He didn't. Julian withdrew his hand slowly and began to cry but still Kristof didn't move.

'This is quite a turnaround Kristof, isn't it?' I observed. 'All the needy longings that were in you are now in Julian and yet somehow you can't respond. I wonder why you're finding it so difficult to do so? This is what you've been asking for – for Julian to show you how much he loves you and wants you.'

I waited for Kristof to say something but he still sat there silent, so I continued.

'It makes me think back to when you talked about your father leaving. You said your mother turned to you for comfort and that it felt like her needs squeezed out all of yours. Maybe it's hard to imagine a relationship where two people can respond to each other, where both of you could, at times, be needy and vulnerable?'

Kristof looked interested and nodded.

'So perhaps whilst there's been something terrible about Julian having been previously so withdrawn, at the same time it's protected you from feeling the burden of his need. Like you felt burdened by your mother?'

To my surprise, Kristof didn't respond but Julian said, 'I've always known that Kristof finds it hard to take on things I want.'

'That's rubbish!' Kristof exploded. 'I've always been there for you.'

Julian looked at him but Kristof turned away. 'Do you remember when I got made redundant and I was in such a mess?'

'Yes. Of course. I was the one supporting you.'

'Actually, Kristof, you were so tough. Really tough. Telling me to get a grip and "man up". That's probably when I gave up the idea that you could ever really care for me.'

'Such rubbish. So you're saying it's my fault you don't want a child or any commitments?'

'I don't think that's what Julian is saying, Kristof. I think he's been trying to explore and acknowledge the source of his own issues but he's also saying that you have your own part to play. It's difficult for both of you to really recognise that this is a shared problem. That moment of disappointment when you were made redundant, Julian, and you felt Kristof couldn't respond, was that, perhaps, when you finally shut down what was already just a sliver of hope inside you that someone would come if you called?'

'Yes,' Julian agreed, 'I stopped having expectations so I wouldn't be disappointed again and then I felt, "Why should I say yes when *you* wanted things?"'

Kristof looked up and over at Julian and I felt something more hopeful was happening. I knew it was the end of the session but I felt an urgency to say something that would hold them until the following week.

'Neither of you are going to be able to meet each other's desires completely but the relationship exists in the trying. Some of these attempts to connect and respond to each other will work and some won't but it's the persistence to keep going, to keep asking and relating, that makes a relationship grow and not wither and die.'

I didn't know what would happen next, I never do. Will a couple find a way through or will they cross that mysterious line that beyond which lies separation? However long I've worked, however many hours I've spent in the consulting room, it is always impossible to know whether a couple, when they hit the crux of their conflicts, will travel on together or part.

But though it was touch and go for many weeks, Julian and Kristof seemed to hang in there. Slowly, a profound shift developed in the balance of the give and take. Julian began to recognise his own needs and desires; it seemed he stopped projecting them all into Kristof who, though it was a struggle, was also becoming less and less fearful of Julian collapsing onto him as his mother had when he was young. This was a huge change in their dynamic, a move away from projective identification to each being more fully themselves in the relationship. We call this kind of development 'taking back projections' where partners reintegrate and 'own' feelings which have previously been denied and then pushed into their partner. Once couples begin to make this kind of change, they can find a new way of being together and for Julian and

Kristof this allowed them to be more vulnerable, leading to a closeness that had hitherto been avoided.

But this change brought out into the open another whole area of difficulty, which, up until now, had been running like an underground river in spate – hidden but extremely powerful. Painfully, but together, we came to understand that neither of them had any real conviction they could make things work between them. They believed that being gay precluded them from having a loving, long-term relationship. It was as though the homophobia and stereotyping they'd experienced all around them was also inside them, poisoning and undermining their belief they could make something good and lasting together. Bringing this out into the light made this fear less powerful and, although they decided not to discuss the thorny issue of children for 12 months, by the time I last saw them, they'd already begun the process of adoption.

THE FATES CONSPIRE, AND RAPUNZEL LETS DOWN HER HAIR

It was January and approaching my husband's birthday. I had no idea what to get him and he was providing me with no suggestions. I noticed he'd propped on his desk a postcard that he'd bought of a linocut he'd seen at a small exhibition near King's Cross. As he clearly admired it, I decided to see if I could buy the original. The etching was of a woman bent and laden, leading a horse along the canal towpath on a winter's day. It was particularly evocative because my husband had previously written a book, *The Water Road*, about a journey through England's inland waterways. Coincidentally, he'd also recently been teaching himself how to make lino prints and this black-and-white picture echoed some of his own work.

It took some time to find the contact details of the artist, Chris Slaney, but when I did, I began an email correspondence regarding a possible purchase. I told Chris why I thought my husband would like the print and he asked for his name. When I gave it he immediately wrote back, excitedly informing me that he'd read *The Water Road* the previous year and the book had inspired him to make the print. I was astonished and excited as I knew my husband would enjoy this story and it would make the present even more meaningful. It set me to pondering that grey area between mere coincidence and deeper unconscious connections.

The following day, I had an enquiry from a prospective patient called Jackson. Could I see him quite urgently? He was in despair as his wife had left him and life felt very dark. His email said he'd got my name from Mr X, who had recommended me. I immediately recognised the name as Mr X was a well-known TV personality. Strangely, I'd never met him and nor did I remember knowing anyone who had.

Jackson was very tall – so tall, in fact, that he had to bend his head as he came through the door into my office in Queen Anne Street. He was rake thin with a bony, aristocratic face that was open and engaging. I warmed to him immediately and his story quickly elicited my sympathies. He told me that he'd known his wife, Carla, for nearly 20 years. They'd met at university and married soon after graduation. He had felt they were well suited and had made each other very happy, though they hadn't had children – Carla, he told me, had felt their lives together were already richly fulfilling and rewarding. Jackson had respected her preference to remain childless but now, at 41, she had suddenly become pregnant by another man and left him. Understandably, he felt shell-shocked and mystified by these events.

Jackson's story wasn't entirely unfamiliar. Over the years, I've seen several patients who have been devastated by revelations and events that seem to come out of the blue. There was the woman whose husband suddenly vanished, abandoning her and his two teenage children (he was found much later, living with his young lover in Thailand) and the deeply sad case of the woman whose husband had, without any warning, drowned himself. Jackson, like both of these patients, had no prior inkling to what was going on and I could see he was utterly confused and desperately reliving the past to try to find the clues he felt he'd missed with Carla.

Soon after Jackson came to see me, a colleague asked if I might take a referral. He had seen a couple who'd now broken up and he wanted to refer the woman, who was very distressed about the ending of the relationship. Her name was Grace and I arranged to meet her the following week.

When Grace arrived, I was immediately struck by her ethereal beauty. She appeared at my door like an illustration from a fairy tale. Her hair was honey blonde and pinned up carelessly so that luxurious ringlets framed her face and tumbled down onto her shoulders like Rapunzel. She'd only been married eight months and yet her dreams were already dashed. Her husband Dylan had left her, saying he'd made a terrible mistake in marrying her.

'He claims he still loves me but he wants to be with a man. He *says* he's sorry but apparently he's now gay. Nine months ago, he didn't know? And now he does? And he's "sorry"?!'

She berated herself bitterly in the session, just as Jackson had done. 'How could I not have known? No one else is surprised. My friends say they always knew – it was so obvious he was gay. Did I have my eyes closed? Why couldn't I see what everyone else did?'

I felt very warm towards Grace; she seemed so sad and lost. She was 34 years old and feared she'd never meet anyone else or have children now. She felt Dylan had almost certainly robbed her of having babies. We talked for an hour and then Grace left, agreeing to come and see me the following week at the same time. Then the buzzer for my next session went.

Bounding up the stairs came Jackson and, as he entered, I was struck by the similarity of their stories. Both had been left and neither saw it coming. Both were not only grieving their marriage but also felt humiliated and preoccupied with the consequent loss of the chance to become parents. It felt very strange. Another coincidence.

Jackson and Grace settled down to their respective therapies. Every week, Grace would leave my office and Jackson would enter ten minutes later. For nearly two hours I listened to their experiences and their feelings and was consistently struck at how profoundly their stories echoed across the two sessions. I began to wonder if they'd like each other and whether they'd find solace in each other's company. I idly fantasised that they might bump into each other on the stairs one day and somehow, as in a movie, connect. Perhaps they could give each other the children they both longed for?

A few months later, spring had drifted back into London. The trees had that particularly pleasing lime-green leaf and, as I walked towards Queen Anne Street, the air smelled of the new season. Mid-morning came, the buzzer went and Grace arrived with her hair down around her face. Her skin looked warmer somehow and something spring-like also seemed to be inhabiting her.

'I've been wanting to tell you something.' She paused. 'I've met someone. It happened in February. I don't know why I didn't tell you sooner. To be truthful, I think I felt a bit awkward.' She paused again. 'I haven't told anyone, actually.'

My mind raced. Was it Jackson? Could it be Jackson she was seeing? I was so caught up in the chain of coincidences that for a moment my imagination ran riot. But then reality intruded into my musings and I remembered that only last week, Jackson had been bemoaning his difficulty in meeting someone new, saying that he still didn't feel attracted to any-one and couldn't stop fantasising that Carla would come back to him.

'I wonder why it feels awkward, Grace?' I asked.

'Well, he's a bit famous; you'll probably have heard of him. And he's married. So . . .' and she trailed off.

I waited, saying nothing.

After a while, she began to talk, explaining that her new lover had two young children. I listened rather sceptically as she told me how sorry he professed to be for dragging her into this tricky situation. He was apparently very aware that she was still getting over her marriage to Dylan.

'To be really truthful, I'm not sure how I feel about it all. I'm not even sure I really like him. Of course, I'm flattered by the attention but I feel a bit bad about his wife . . . and his kids.'

'But maybe a bit excited too?' I asked and she nodded.

Her face slightly flushed and her tone slightly giggly, she talked about how he seemed totally paranoid. He was very fearful they'd be seen and that the tabloids would find out he was having an affair. The previous week, he had come to see her in her third-floor flat and had insisted, even though it was broad daylight, that she pull down the blinds, just in case someone with a long lens was peeping in. I wondered aloud if the fact that it was so cloak and dagger quite suited her right now but she protested that it wasn't what she wanted and she knew it was wrong.

I was beginning to think how interesting it was that she seemed, once again, to have found a man who couldn't really commit to her and who wasn't being honest. And there was also something about secrets that seemed to link her experiences. Firstly, there was Dylan, who'd not disclosed the confusion he felt about his sexuality, and now here was someone who was married and who therefore very clearly needed to keep their relationship private. I was chewing over how to begin to explore this with her when she giggled.

'Do you want to know who it is? Shall I tell you?'

I sat silently, I was curious but why was she tantalising me in this way? I wondered.

'It's Mr X,' she said.

After that revelation, I didn't really speak for what remained of the session. Mr X! The same Mr X who'd recommended Jackson to me. I felt confused and a bit alarmed. In my work, confidentiality and clear boundaries are absolutely essential to protect my patients and now it felt as if something was breaching those boundaries. It was as if Mr X had somehow got right inside my consulting room. Suddenly, it felt as if *I* was the one with a secret. I pondered this after Grace left. I was shaken by the enormous coincidence that Grace and Jackson, whose sessions with me were separated by a mere ten minutes, were also suddenly connected through him. And as this was another coincidence in a series of them, I felt a little spooked.

Both Freud and Jung, those great fathers of psychoanalysis, were very curious about coincidences and speculated about their links to the paranormal. Freud, despite his deeply religious upbringing, never came to a settled conclusion about whether there was a spiritual world and, fearing he'd undermine the scientific basis of psychoanalysis, he largely avoided the whole topic. Jung, on the other hand, developed a theoretical framework that incorporated mystical elements, which went beyond the known and provable. He called the phenomenon of coincidence, synchronicity and described it as an essentially mysterious connection between the personal psyche and the material world, based on the fact both of these are forms of energy.

Personally, I lean towards Freud's more rationalist approach and consider the words of Helene Deutsch – one of the first female psychoanalysts – to be very apposite: 'Occult powers are to be sought in the depth of the psychic life, and psychoanalysis is destined to clarify this problem in the same manner in which it has previously clarified other "mysterious" happenings in the human psyche.'*

* Helene Deutsch, *The Therapeutic Process, the Self, and Female Psychology: Collected Psychoanalytic Papers* (Routledge, 1999).

For instance, one patient came to me saying that she feared from her dreams that she was demonic. She dreamt of buried bodies, of her teeth turning to fangs and of alien monsters erupting from her chest. It was alarming for her and sometimes the dreams were so graphic it was alarming for me. But careful analysis of these dreams revealed themselves to be infantile imaginings that came from her deeply repressed childhood rage. Eventually we understood that it wasn't the rage that was the issue for her but rather the way her family situation had required her, as a very young child, to repress it, leaving her feeling guilty and unnatural for feeling so angry. Now the only way these emotions could be expressed was through her dreams.

By the time Grace arrived the following week, I felt much less alarmed. Yes, here was a series of strange coincidences but although London is a big city, I knew from experience that it could also be a small world, so I focused my attention on what meaning this affair with a married man had for Grace and why she was excited by it. In the session, she talked to me about the deep connection she felt to Mr X and how, although their relationship seemed fated, she felt that she'd known him forever. She chattered on about their plans for a night away and as I listened silently her mood began to shift from excited to reflective.

'Why is it', she complained, 'that every man I meet seems to be gay or married?'

We discussed how this affair with Mr X held considerable jeopardy for her, particularly given the recent rejection by her husband, and I wondered to myself why she was taking this risk so lightly.

As it turned out, the affair with Mr X fizzled out quite quickly. His work took him overseas and they agreed that their relationship couldn't really go anywhere. But my thoughts about Grace and the partners she was choosing began to develop further as she then embarked upon a series of relationships that all ended suddenly. She'd begin to date someone in an excited and enthusiastic way but quite quickly she'd find them too keen or they'd abruptly drop her. She also began to tell me about her love life before her marriage to Dylan. All through her twenties she had avoided getting involved with anyone. She'd had many one-night stands but somehow either she or her date didn't pursue it further. Her first proper relationship had been with Oscar, an older, clever and successful man, whom she'd met at a conference in Rome. He lived in Copenhagen so they began a long-distance affair that lasted four years. Eventually, however, that too fizzled out and soon afterwards she found out that Oscar had got married and had a child. I wondered if she and Oscar had ever discussed living together and she told me no, not really. Oscar had sometimes joked they should get married but she'd never taken him seriously. But Grace was, apparently, now ready for something serious. She talked often about her age and how her friends were becoming settled with partners and having babies. She dated furiously, bemoaning the problems of the internet and how all the men she met were jerks or boring. Mostly she'd dismiss them out of hand but occasionally she'd become excited about someone – and I would notice that this 'someone' always seemed a bit unsuitable or unavailable.

'The fates are against me,' she complained, 'I'm so unlucky.'

But it wasn't about luck and it was no coincidence that she was struggling to get into a serious relationship.

Of course, chance and coincidence play their part in people finding love but from my perspective, it's by no means the most powerful force at work. The romantic idea that you and your partner were destined to meet is a charming, sweet notion but, frankly, pretty unlikely, and the myth that on Halloween, with the aid of a brush, apple and candle, you will see your future husband's ghostly image in the mirror is clearly unproved. Nevertheless, these myths and superstitions relating to finding love are powerful and enduring in all cultures. I remember, in my early teens, when buses had conductors with silver ticket machines slung around their necks, staring intently at the letters and numbers on this tiny piece of paper for clues to my future love life. How much I longed to know *my* destiny.

But though the fates don't choose our partners, something nearly as mysterious *is* at work – our unconscious. We seem drawn to certain people, we connect, we click. We seem to like their smell, the way they move, the way they laugh. Something attracts us and whilst they may, in actuality, be beautiful, kind and clever, that mysterious something goes beyond these known and visible attributes.

There is a theory, derived from psychoanalysis, about why couples choose each other. It's one that I find not only compelling but which has been borne out by my own clinical experience. This theory suggests that the way we're cared for, handled, loved and nurtured in childhood shapes us. Alongside this direct experience, we also witness and observe the intimate relationships around us. We watch our mothers and our fathers love; we absorb the way our carers treat each other and these influences structure our deepest feelings about intimacy. We learn how safe it is to depend on another human and if it's not safe, we watch our loved ones and learn ways to protect ourselves. All this can leave us with a problem, a problem that we only really confront when we get older and begin love affairs of our own.

We can be popular at school, do well at work and excel at sports but when we love, then the trouble, which began in childhood, comes home to roost. We find ourselves attracted to people whose early experiences dovetail or complement ours. We're powerfully drawn to them as though, at some level, not accessible to our conscious minds, we recognise each other; we feel understood, known. Now, of course, neuroscientists and social scientists would emphasise different reasons for why we fall in love. They'd say it's pheromones and hormones that determine who you fall for. They'd reference evolutionary biology or cite class, social status or a crossover of interests. And whilst I'm sure all of these things are factors, I'm also convinced that a compelling part of falling in love includes things that are deeply unconscious.

Young lovers lie in bed discovering each other's lives and feel weirdly as one. From the superficial excitement at finding out you like the same colour, read the same authors and love the same TV series to listening intently to this new person's feelings about their life, their hopes, their family – something just . . . resonates. Of course, attraction is also affected by looks, accents, jobs, social status, etc., but running alongside all these calculations is what, in our deepest minds, we feel about coupling and love. Grace wasn't unlucky in love; it was no coincidence she kept on connecting with men who let her down – these men simply reflected her own uncertainty about commitment, her own deep ambivalence about letting someone into her heart.

One morning she arrived at the consulting room in an agitated state and I immediately noticed how pale she looked.

'My father's coming to London. He's been living in Sydney with his new wife for the last eight years. I haven't seen him since he moved there. He's coming with her . . . It's going to be awful.'

I had heard very little about her family, apart from the fact that her parents were divorced. She seemed very close to her mother but her relationship with her father was distant and awkward.

'That's a long time not to have seen him,' I commented.

'He's asked me to visit. Several times. I just never wanted to go. He's coming back now because, apparently, her sister is ill.'

'Her sister?' I enquired. 'His second wife's sister?'

'Third wife,' corrected Grace.

She then began to tell me more about her parents' divorce when she was eleven and her brother was seven. She told it in a way that felt as if she'd never thought about it before, as though it had been locked away inside her mind since it happened. She spoke hesitantly, with past and present muddled and the narrative jumbled and confusing. Her father and mother, she claimed, had seemed happy and never argued, so the divorce had come as a total shock.

'I haven't always been distanced from Dad. When I was little, we were really close. He was funny and played with me and my brother much more than Mum ever did.'

'Do you have memories of when he left?'

'I was devastated, actually. I remember feeling sick and frightened. Mum told me not to cry. She always said he was a shit and didn't deserve any tears.'

'A shit?' I questioned.

'Basically, he left me for another woman.'

I was struck by her Freudian slip; Grace had meant to say that he'd left her *mother* for another woman.

'Perhaps your father's betrayal of your mother felt like it was a betrayal of you?' I asked.

'I think he was probably having affairs all the time.' She paused and then spoke very slowly, again as if recalling things for the first time. 'I remember being taken on drives and being left in the car. I hated it. I was always scared because he'd be a long, long time. When he came back it would be dark. Then he'd take me to Toys'R'Us before we went home.' She frowned. 'When I was older, he took me to Hennes to buy clothes. He bought me a lot of clothes.'

Grace then began to cry but instantly fought against it, pushing the tears back down until she had control.

'Actually, I hate him now,' she said. 'He's a selfish cunt. He was obviously fucking someone whilst I sat in the car. Jesus, what a bastard.'

'You feel very angry, Grace. I think it feels like he betrayed you.'

'He's just a cunt!' Grace repeated.

'You're expressing a lot of anger but not any hurt. It sounds like you were very frightened and confused by all this as a child. Perhaps the anger protects you from these other feelings?'

Grace nodded and I saw her eyes brim with tears again.

In the following weeks, we slowly began to understand more about her difficulties with intimacy and commitment. We explored how there were two contradictory feelings inside her that could easily be evoked if she began to get close to a lover. The first feeling was her fear of losing love and being rejected, and it seemed the source of this fear related to her childhood loss of her father. She'd adored him but often felt, even before he left, that her connection to him was precarious. Her father had been exciting and seductive but then he'd drop her for work or a lover, meaning that Grace had never felt truly secure.

'I think I always felt I bored him. He'd play with us but then he'd look irritated with me and he'd go out. I always felt anxious about that. That he'd leave me behind.'

She told me that when he did finally leave home, she rarely saw him, though from time to time he'd turn up and sweep her off her feet, only to drop her again, leaving her bereft.

The second feeling that seemed to be interfering with making a serious commitment to a man was that, whilst she worried about being left, she also feared getting too close and could, quite easily, feel suffocated and long for her own space. She would often describe this as being 'peopled out'. I began to wonder if unconsciously she'd married Dylan *because* he was ambivalent about her; that his ambivalence, because he was gay, echoed her own.

She then began to talk a great deal about her mother and I could see how intense their relationship was. I wondered whether this was the other side of the coin. Did this intensity with her mother, which made her feel suffocated, get re-evoked in her relationships with lovers? It was clear that intimate relationships could easily make her feel claustrophobic.

One morning, as we drew near to the August break, Grace started her session by complaining about her holiday plans. 'You know I told you about me going away with my friend Chloe and her brother Tom? We've rented this flat in Mykonos.'

I nodded.

'Well, you won't believe it, but my mother has rented an Airbnb practically right across the street. Which is ridiculous because it's right in the middle of the old town, which she'll hate. This is practically the first summer holiday I've had in ages without her. I don't want to be mean to her but she's not going to enjoy it anyway. She hates hot places and I don't think she'll like the clubbing much either!' Her laughter died away and she paused. 'I can't tell her not to come, she'd be too upset.'

I was struck at how intrusive her mother was. Couldn't she see that she'd be unwelcome and that barging into her 35-year-old daughter's holiday was a little inappropriate? This incident gave me a clearer picture of the relationship between them and I began to see how Grace could feel that it wasn't just her father who put his own needs first. But then I also asked myself why Grace wasn't more assertive with her mother. Why didn't she gently explain that she wanted to go alone? It seemed as if it was impossible for her to say anything to her mother that smacked of rejection or might start an argument. It reminded me of the way her mother had instructed her not to cry over her father's desertion and how, dutifully, Grace had therefore suppressed her feelings.

I also began to notice the way Grace was treating me. She was mostly a very solicitous patient, enquiring how I was doing at the start of each appointment, despite my never giving more than a discouraging brief nod. It wasn't that I minded her asking but I wanted her to understand that in therapy she didn't need to follow these social protocols. She'd also look worried when I responded to her in a compassionate way, almost as though it was me who was hurting rather than her. If I looked concerned, she'd become agitated and reassure me she was fine. She paid her bill literally minutes after I sent it to her and she always kept an eye on the timing of the session, never leaving it to me to say that it was time to end.

It began to dawn on me that perhaps she felt I needed protecting in some way; sometimes she even seemed to treat me as though I was the needy, fragile one, not her. I recognised this as the transference – was she recreating with me the kind of relationship she had with her mother?

Understanding the transference and countertransference is central to the way I work and, indeed, to the work of all psychoanalytic therapists. The transference refers to the way attitudes and feelings about a relationship from the past are recreated in the relationship between a patient and their therapist. Whilst countertransference refers to the feelings a patient may stir up in the therapist and how these might relate to the re-enactment of a pattern of relationship derived usually from childhood experience. In Grace's case, it began to be evident that feelings about her mother's fragility were being 'transferred' onto me and I could see that she was convinced that I needed to be handled with kid gloves. This really helped me get a sense of how deeply she feared upsetting her mother.

Then something else shone further light on childhood events that seemed to be shaping her current love life. As Grace's curiosity about herself grew, she wanted to know more about her childhood but it seemed there were many things she couldn't remember. It was almost as if there were gaps she couldn't fill, and they began to worry her. Finally, she worked up the courage to have a conversation with her mother whilst on a weekend visit to her aunt in Norfolk. It was a sunny day and the three of them sat in the garden drinking Pimm's and talking about the past. After an hour of them jointly bitching about her father, she asked her mother about her birth and her mother told her tearfully that she'd been hospitalised with postnatal depression soon after Grace was born. And this had happened again when Grace's brother arrived, two years later.

Was this at the root of why Grace was so protective of her mother? In my mind, I visualised a two-year-old desperately missing her mum. I imagined that Grace, in a child's way, may have sensed her mother's fragility and been very frightened by it. Had she then become hypersensitive to her mother's moods? Had she tried her absolute best to prevent her mother becoming sad and leaving again? What a burden this must have been for a little toddler.

Over some weeks, we talked about these aspects of her childhood and how some of the feelings she had about her mother were being repeated with me. Gradually, this seemed to make a difference and I sensed that she was less depressed and more hopeful – she'd made some important connections with her past that allowed her greater insight into her present and seemed to make her feel she could shape her future differently.

Making links between one thing and another is the daily work of a psychoanalytic therapist. Threading together seemingly random thoughts, behaviour and events helps to make sense of a patient's inner world and to bring some meaning to what is confusing and fragmented. Being alive to these links is perhaps the nearest we can get to apprehending the unconscious. That part of the mind that runs like an underground river shaping all we think, all we do and how we love.

Unfortunately, patients, particularly early in their treatment, can sometimes be sceptical about these links and, at times, positively scornful. The idea that their conscious self isn't necessarily in the driving seat can feel quite alarming. However, at some point in the therapy, there's often a shift in attitude and that's when genuine breakthroughs become possible. Patients then bring their own insights about their dreams, their pre-occupations and their day-to-day lives.

I remember one patient who was extremely anxious when her long-term partner told her, now he was retired, that he wanted to buy a flat in London so that he could visit galleries and go to the theatre – pleasures he'd missed greatly since moving to the country. The couple lived in the middle of a national park, surrounded by mountains and lakes, and though my patient's husband had often spoken of his desire for a London pied-à-terre, he had never acted on it. She had been sleepless all week and, despite her partner's reassurance that he wanted her company on these trips, she felt convinced it was otherwise and that he was really telling her that this was a precursor to their relationship ending.

I was puzzled by the strength and depth of this anxiety. I couldn't make head or tail of it until some weeks later when she began to talk about her parents' separation and how it had followed a heated and protracted dispute over purchasing a villa in France. Her French father desperately wanted to spend some of his retirement back in his homeland but her English mother put her foot down and resisted fiercely. Her parents fought over this for a year and then abruptly divorced. Suddenly, the connection between this memory of her parents' separation, which she'd found deeply traumatic, and her current worries about her own relationship became clear. And this link, which had hitherto been unconscious, helped her to understand her panic at her partner's suggestion.

Both Jackson and Grace seemed similarly to be in a process of development, making connections between their pasts and their present challenges. Jackson had slowly emerged from his grief and now he'd met a woman he liked called Veronica. He had been bored at work for some time and, feeling more confident again, had applied for a new job and was thrilled when he got it. It was quite a promotion and meant that, at last, he was doing what he'd always wanted to do. The only issue was his hours were less flexible and his 9.30am appointment was no longer possible. Could I see him earlier, at 8.30am, he enquired? I told him I didn't have an earlier time free but, as the session with him progressed, I thought to myself that Grace, being freelance, might be able to come an hour later. The following week, I asked her if she'd mind changing to 9.30am and she readily agreed.

One morning, about three weeks after the swap, she came into her session flushed with anger. 'That guy. That guy you see before me. The guy who used to come *after* me.' She laughed scornfully. 'What's his problem? He always gives me a really dirty look and just now he shut the door on me as I was coming in. I presume it's cos of him you asked me to change time?'

I was rather taken aback by this and didn't respond immediately. Grace just sat there looking cross with her arms folded, challenging me.

'Perhaps it feels as if I've put his needs first, Grace, and messed you around?'

'Well, you kinda have, haven't you?' She paused. 'You got me to change times so it was more convenient for him.'

'Was it inconvenient for you?' I asked.

'That's not the point,' she responded. 'It's just not fair of you to have got *me* to inconvenience myself for *him*.'

I felt surprised and wrong-footed. The reasonable and emollient Grace had disappeared and, in her stead, sat this angry, demanding child.

It took some time for Grace to calm down and for us to explore her feelings about the swap. It was clear that I hadn't spent enough time checking out whether it was really OK for her; her tendency to be amenable and compliant with me hadn't been properly explored and now she felt that, once again, her own needs had been overridden in favour of someone else's.

'My mum always puts herself first. My father is a massive bloody narcissist and gets his own way . . . and here you are, doing the same thing.'

I didn't point out that her accusation was unfair and irrational: the swap wasn't about my needs but about Jackson's. I understood that at this moment, she felt as if I, like her parents, had somehow made her secondary.

After that, Grace began to start each session by talking about Jackson – she didn't know his name but called him 'Mr Big'. She'd come early and ring my buzzer, interrupting Jackson's session despite my having asked her, as I asked all my patients, not to come more than ten minutes before the session time.

'How's Mr Big, your favourite patient?' she'd joke in a sing-song voice.

But when I tried to explore her rivalry with him, she'd

dismiss me and say she was only joking and not everything was that serious.

Some weeks later, Jackson was in the middle of talking about his fears about moving in with Veronica when the buzzer went. I glanced at the clock: it was 9.15am. I looked at Jackson, who said, rather bitterly, 'She's keen.' I felt furious with her. This was intolerable and couldn't go on.

In the ten-minute break between the two of them I gathered myself and thought about what I was going to say, then I opened my door and beckoned Grace in. She took off her coat with her back to me and sat down, staring defiantly.

'Grace,' I said, sounding calmer than I felt. 'I need to be clear. You're *not* to come early. I've asked before but if you continue to ring the bell early, then we'll need to rethink your sessions.' She looked at me anxiously. 'I'll have to move you to a different time,' I explained.

'But that *is* my time. The other time.' Then she put her head down on her knees and burst into tears.

After that session, Grace stopped coming early. It took some weeks to unpick what had been going on and we gradually understood that she'd been testing me to see whether I would reject her if she behaved badly. So when I had simply 'told her off', she'd felt hugely relieved because she'd feared her behaviour might result in my 'sacking' her. Gradually, it also emerged that this hostility she felt towards Jackson was connected to a belief that her mother had always favoured her brother – she believed that I preferred Jackson to her. She was able to acknowledge how jealous she felt of her sibling and this led to her connecting to long-forgotten feelings about his birth and how this had triggered her mother leaving her to go into hospital. This ancient hostility and fear, which was deep inside her and hard to reach, had led to this irrational resentment towards Jackson, whose name she didn't even know.

The work continued. Grace came regularly to her sessions and soon I began to hear about Marcus, whom she had met on a work trip. Months passed and the relationship seemed to be developing. She talked about their ups and downs and many times I thought she'd break the relationship off but gradually he became a fixture in her life. Rapunzel was letting down her hair and letting Marcus into her life.

Some months later, I'd just got back from holiday in America and, jet-lagged, I slept through my alarm. It was 8.31am and I hurried along Welbeck Street, late for Jackson, when I saw him outside, waiting. He lifted one arm in greeting and smiled warmly as I fiddled for my key.

'I've got some news,' he said as he disappeared into the loo.

I walked into my consulting room, straightened the cushions and soon Jackson came in, removing his jacket as he entered.

He smiled. 'Veronica's pregnant!'

Fifty minutes later he departed and I picked up my iPhone to read a message from Grace: *Running late – Had to go to doctor.*

Twenty minutes later, the buzzer sounded and Grace appeared, pink-faced and sweaty from the journey.

'Guess what? I'm pregnant!' she announced.

Freud theorised that there is probably no such thing as an accident or a coincidence. Whilst we may be ignorant of something at one level, at another level, feelings, ideas, events and experiences are always being unconsciously communicated and assimilated. Perhaps we 'know' things at many different levels? Sometimes we're able to know fully and consciously whilst at other times, when 'knowing' might be too painful or our attention is elsewhere, we find ourselves in a state of 'not knowing'.

Was I particularly alert during this period? Did I notice confluences and concurrences that at other times I'm blind to? Or were all these coincidences simply that? Happenstance, random events coming together that had no meaning, neither mystical nor unconscious?

BEAR LEARNS ABOUT BEAUTY
AND THE BEAST

A man called Bear came to see me because he was having a difficult time in his relationship. He sat down heavily on my sofa and stared at me dolefully until I encouraged him to tell me why he'd come. He seemed reticent and talked evasively about his partner and children and his job in IT, which he found dull but paid the bills. He had a lopsided grin when he could manage one, enormous brown hands and wild curly hair. He was rather attractive apart from the smell of damp sadness that emanated from him.

Eventually, I said, 'It seems you have some difficulty telling me what is really troubling you.'

He looked away and out of the window and said, 'I can't stand the way she sighs.'

'Sighs?' I asked. I wasn't sure I'd heard correctly.

He was silent again and then, raising his head, he nodded and said, 'Yes, she sighs.'

Though I encouraged him several times to tell me more, he seemed reluctant to expand and I heard nothing more about the sighing in that first session. As I travelled home on the bus I wondered what it could mean. I knew how my husband's sighs could affect me, how alert I could be to this little signal from him that might indicate he was tired or perhaps displeased about something. And I knew that I could also be given to sighing and thought about how there was sometimes a kind of lovely relief in doing so.

When Bear came back to see me the following week, he said, 'I told my partner this evening that I was going off to see you. She was in the kitchen feeding the dog. I asked her if she wanted to come. She didn't look up. She just sighed.' He paused. 'I wanted to hit her. I'm afraid I might hit her if she sighs like that again.'

A shiver of alarm went through me; I could hear the rage and spite in his voice and I could hear it more loudly than I could hear his fear. I asked him what stopped him from hitting her and if he ever had. He shook his head and stared at his shoes.

'I've never hit her and I don't think I ever would but sometimes I feel as though I'm going to explode into little pieces.' And then he apologised for what he'd just said and reassured me that he wasn't dangerous, that I needn't worry.

For the rest of the session, he talked in a monotone about his job and I suddenly felt tired and sleepy. Feeling sleepy is an exceedingly rare thing for me – mostly, when my patients talk, I'm fully there with them, attentive to everything they say and alert to how they look and how they react to the things I might suggest to them. I'm taking them in with my whole self and stretching out to connect with them. So, when I feel sleepy in a session, it's something to take seriously and I ask myself what it means and whether my patient is unconsciously communicating something. From my own experience and from the wisdom of others, I've learnt that feeling sleepy can sometimes be a sign that the patient has a great deal of repressed anger and that the consequence of this repression is a general flattening of their manner and their behaviour, suppressing the livelier part of themselves. Obviously, in my reflections, I must exclude the obvious, such as my sleepiness being due to jet lag or a particularly bad night's sleep, but neither of those were factors on that day with Bear. Towards the end of the session, I thought about how odd it was that he had started with such violence and yet now he seemed utterly lifeless and flat.

'I think you're afraid of the violent feelings your wife stirs up in you and that you work hard to damp them down rather than understand what causes them,' I suggested.

He nodded and said that he'd been told that before by the psychologist who'd helped him with his drinking. I was surprised because he hadn't mentioned he'd had problems with alcohol but now he told me that his drinking had spiralled out of control after his first son was born and the previous year he'd spent six weeks in rehab away from the family. He'd been dry now for 14 months.

'Did your feelings about your wife's sighing start after you stopped drinking?' I asked.

He nodded. The session was coming to an end and as he slowly gathered his things and left my office, I thought about his anger and wondered if he'd used alcohol to damp down his fury. Was something now coming to the surface in his relationship with his wife that had previously been masked when he was drinking?

The following week, Bear came early and sat patiently outside my room for 20 minutes but when the session started, he seemed to have nothing to say and we sat in silence for some time. After a bit, his phone buzzed and he picked it up off the sofa where it sat beside him. I watched as he read the message before looking back at me.

'She's outside. She wants to come in.' He looked at me, panicked, and for a moment I wondered who the hell was outside; it felt like someone dangerous, someone out to get him. Then it dawned on me – it was his wife.

'What shall I say?' he asked, his eyes wide with alarm.

'Do you want her to come in?' I asked.

'Don't tell her what I told you,' he said fiercely, rising from the couch. 'I'm going downstairs to see her.' And he got up and left.

I waited in my room, wondering what would happen next. I imagined her bursting into my office, demanding to know what was going on. The way he'd reacted to the text made me feel she must be quite scary. After a while, I heard voices outside and then footsteps on the stairs. My door opened and Bear reappeared, followed by a small, slight woman with beautiful brown eyes and curly brown hair, who smiled at me nervously as she took a seat. She was wearing a long, green dress peppered with tiny white flowers and as she sat down, I noticed her dainty brown feet and the tiny gold chain she wore around her ankle.

'I'm really sorry for just turning up. I felt bad about not coming last week when Bear asked.' She paused, shook her curls and looked at me questioningly. 'But obviously if it isn't cool, I can split now.' She looked from me to Bear with her head angled to the side, waiting expectantly for a sign whether she was welcome. How meek she seemed; so different from what I'd expected.

We talked for a while about what they wanted – did they both want couple therapy and was Bear comfortable with her being in the session? I said that I thought they needed to go away and think through what was best. Then they could let me know and we could see how to proceed.

She shook my hand as they left and apologised again for turning up without warning. I wondered if I'd see her again.

Three days later, Bear emailed me to say that Saffron wasn't coming – she thought that he should continue with me on his own.

At the next session, I was quite taken aback. Bear looked different; wearing forest-green yoga pants, he suddenly seemed much less conventional.

'I'm really sorry about last week,' he began. 'I thought I wanted her to come and then I really didn't. She can't know what I told you about the sighing. She'd be upset, furious, she'd go mad if she knew what I'd said to you.'

I noted how fearful his response seemed. Was he concerned that Saffron would be hurt or was he worried she'd be angry?

'You talk about Saffron as though you're very scared of her or perhaps of upsetting her? It's as though you fear she'd break or explode if you said anything at all negative or critical.' As I spoke, I knew there was a disparity between how Bear experienced Saffron and how she seemed to me. I couldn't quite square the person who'd come to the session the previous week – who seemed neither fragile nor fierce – with the terror Bear was expressing. Neither did it seem that Bear had told me anything about her that could justify his anxious concern. Something didn't add up.

There are many moments in couple therapy when the therapist is confronted with a disparity between how one partner sees the other and how, in actuality, they really are. I remember one couple where the woman, Yolande, an elegant and accomplished person in her mid-fifties came to see me one early summer. Her husband was in the armed forces and away on tour and we agreed, rather unusually, that she would come alone until he returned to the UK in September. She had a rich and interesting life and spent a great deal of time caring for others, which she found rewarding and interesting. However, she was deeply disappointed in her marriage and over the few months we met alone, she complained bitterly about her husband. As we talked, I got a picture of a rather cold and uncaring man. She wept about his lack of real interest in her and her life and she raged angrily about his authoritarian and controlling personality. She told me how critical he was of her – her cooking, her clothes and the company she kept – painting a portrait of a man obsessed with his status and how the world saw them as a couple. By the end of the summer, I had a very vivid picture in my mind of her husband, a picture which reminded me of the character Soames in the *Forsyte Saga* novels. Cold, cruel, inadequate and very self-important. A beast of a man, not an attractive picture at all. So, it was with some trepidation that I arranged to meet him individually before we began the joint couple work.

September came and into my office walked a tall, slightly balding and very upright man. He smiled at me warmly and began his narrative by telling me how Yolande had spoken so well of me and how much he'd been looking forward to coming. I was taken aback; here was someone completely different from the man I'd pictured. Not cold and arrogant at all but instead gracious and, surprisingly, given his rank, humble. Yolande had seen her husband through a lens that was distorted by her own internal world. And yet, though Yolande's husband wasn't the Soames she painted him to be, over time, I came to see that there *were* actually aspects of him that confirmed her view. It was just a lot more complex and nuanced than the picture she held of him in her mind. Neither Beauty, nor Beast.

It seemed this distortion was going on inside Bear as he continued to experience Saffron as both fragile and frightening. We would discuss how he might talk more directly to her about his feelings but, when it came to it, he was never able to do so and so nothing seemed to change. The weeks passed and though he persisted in talking about her sighs, we seemed unable to make much sense of it. Why, I wondered, did the sighing get to him so badly? I could see that often he was silently irritable with her and we regularly discussed this anger he had. Gradually, he was able to acknowledge his own unhappy feelings but he still felt murderous when she sighed.

One Tuesday morning, Bear came in looking exhausted; his normal springy mop of hair looked as depressed and flattened as he did. He told me he'd been up all night worrying because Saffron had snapped at him and he hadn't slept a wink.

'It started cos I forgot to buy bread on the way home from work. She said that I didn't listen to her and that I was thoughtless. In front of the children, too.' He paused briefly and looked at me, hoping, I think, for sympathy, and then continued with his tale of woe. Saffron was unfair on him; Saffron was unkind to him; Saffron never said thank you; Saffron never seemed to look out for his welfare. As I listened, I thought to myself that her comments had sounded really quite mild.

'You often feel that Saffron is raging at you, Bear. I wonder why?'

'She hasn't forgiven me.'

'Forgiven you?'

'For missing Arlo's birth.'

He then told me with great shame that when his second son was born, he'd been in the pub, drinking after work. Saffron called him to say she thought she was going into labour but, somehow, he didn't leave the pub and when he eventually got home, she'd already gone to the hospital without him. When he arrived at the labour ward, the midwife had sent him back home because he was too drunk. After he told me, we sat in silence and I waited for him to say more.

'Saffron didn't speak to me when she came back with the baby. She wouldn't even let me hold him. Wouldn't have anything to do with me at all,' Bear recounted, his voice breaking. 'When Arlo was a week old, I went and talked to the GP and she arranged for me to go to rehab. Her mother moved in whilst I was in treatment.'

'I wonder how it was when you came home?'

Bear shrugged. 'We never really talked about it.'

This confession gave me a much stronger insight into

their situation and I felt in my own bones the let-down and betrayal Saffron must have felt. To be so careless, to not make it to your own son's birth, that must have stirred up feelings hard to recover from.

'Perhaps her sighing is her way of expressing how upset she still feels, Bear?' I suggested. 'Every time she sighs, I think you hear her berating you for what you did. She sighs and it makes you feel so guilty and bad, and you hate her for it.' Bear looked miserable and nodded. 'It seems you both have difficulties in facing your feelings, perhaps even knowing what they are. And neither of you have felt able to talk things through with each other. You've previously dealt with your emotional pain by anaesthetising yourself with alcohol and perhaps Saffron can only express her feelings by sighing?'

'I just wish she'd be happy. That I could *make* her happy. I used to. If I can't make her happy, what's the point? What's the point of anything?' Bear responded sadly.

It seemed that for Bear and Saffron, heavy breaths, huffs, puffs and sighs was the only language they spoke, and Bear was hyper-alert to these 'tells', his antennae always out for these almost silent 'accusations'.

A few sessions later, he began by telling me he was feeling a little better. He talked about how much the weather could affect his mood and how much he'd enjoyed walking through Regent's Park to my office. He said, 'June is bustin' out all over!' And laughed. I said that I thought he looked like he was bustin' out today too. Then, looking thoughtful, he began to talk about how he wished he could be more spontaneous and freer.

'Spontaneous and free?' I echoed, hoping he would say more about what he meant.

He shrugged his shoulders and I noticed that he held his hands together and then seemed to place them protectively over his crotch.

'Is the spontaneity you long for anything to do with your sexual feelings?' I asked.

He nodded and then he talked about how he and Saffron had woken up early and had sex. It was the first time they'd made love for a long while. Gradually, he explained that when he was drinking their sex life had 'gone down the toilet'. Most of the time, he'd been too drunk in the evenings to have sex and Saffron would be up early before him in the mornings. When he'd come out of rehab, they'd had quite a lot of sex but it just hadn't worked very well, so they'd stopped.

'What was it that didn't work, Bear?' I asked.

He blew out his cheeks and looked uncomfortable but after some moments he told me that Saffron hadn't liked it anymore. She didn't get excited and he couldn't make her come, though he tried and tried.

'This morning, she came. She seemed to be really enjoying it – I thought the kids would hear her she made so much noise.'

'Sighing?' I asked, smiling.

'Yes, sighing! A *lot* of sighing!' he laughed.

We talked then about how much his sense of goodness was dependent on making Saffron happy and how before she was pregnant, whenever something went wrong between them, he could always make her happy in bed. It was how they made up – without words and with their bodies.

After that session, Saffron's sighing didn't anger Bear so much. Things opened up and we began to talk about his fragile sense of his own goodness – his uncertainty about whether he was a good man or a selfish beast.

People repeat patterns. Patterns of relating learnt at the knees of their mothers or fathers. From the work we did together, I came to understand that Bear's parents hadn't been happy together. His father was an angry man, remote and cold, and his mother had often been sad and disappointed. Bear had been hyper-alert to his mother's moods; she'd made the weather in the house. Very occasionally, she made the sun come out but mostly she made black clouds. The strongest image Bear had of his mother was of her watching television in her bedroom on a miniature set which she placed on a tray across her lap. He would knock gently and go in and sit gingerly, perched on the end of the bed, just to be near her. He remembered the blue candlewick bedspread and picking at it with his finger, bored and lonely and fearful she'd find him a nuisance and send him away. He grew up with an abiding sense that he wasn't a delight, that he didn't lift her heart or please her. Deep in his bones, he thought of himself as a burden and feared *he* was the cause of her sadness, *he* was the one who'd disappointed her. Now, he lived in fear of disappointing Saffron. Just as he'd monitored his mother's moods, he had watched Saffron in exactly the same way, fearfully listening out for those black clouds. When Saffron was sunny, when he could make her sigh with delight, he felt like a prince amongst men, happy and proud. Without that assurance, he felt like a beast, angry and dangerous, bad inside.

PART TWO
BETRAYAL

Of course I'll hurt you. Of course you'll hurt me. Of course we will hurt each other. But this is the very condition of existence. To become spring, means accepting the risk of winter. To become presence, means accepting the risk of absence.

—Antoine de Saint-Exupéry, *Manon, Ballerina*

What is betrayal? It nearly always involves lies and it always involves selfishness. The betrayer puts their own interests, wishes and needs first; whilst their loved one had trusted, they would not. To be an adulterer or a traitor is still, in many places in the world a very dangerous thing to be; though in the West, at least, neither offence will bring about dire consequences. No hands will be cut off or eyes gouged out, no banishment enforced. Despite this, we condemn adulterers – revile them in the press and send flowers and love to the cuckold. But imagine if we could get inside their heads, and understand more about both 'victim' and 'perpetrator'?

Perhaps the first betrayal comes, as Freud suggested, when we are confronted with our parents' relationship. The devastating discovery that our beloved parent loves another, leaves most of us uncomfortable in a threesome and many of us unconsciously play out unresolved feelings from that first betrayal in our own love affairs.

When we break our vows, when we attack the bonds of love and trust, are we unconsciously attacking our parents' loving link in our minds? When a woman begins an affair with a married man, is she paying back her mother for coming first with her father? When a man finds a mistress is he triumphing over his big daddy who took his precious mummy from him?

But betrayal isn't all about sex; there are many forms of dishonesty in relationships and all of them undermine the glue that holds our most intimate and meaningful relationships together.

KAMAL DISCOVERS WHO'S BEEN SLEEPING IN HIS BED

'You must be fucking joking. No way . . . absolutely, no fucking way,' Kamal exploded.

Cecily sat there, her face streaked with tears and her chest heaving with unspoken feelings. Kamal began to leave. 'I'm not staying to listen to this. I'm sorry, Susanna.' He rose and made his way towards the door. Then he hesitated, turned back to Cecily and said plaintively, 'Do you want me to go? Do you?' She looked at me and then him and in a quiet, small voice said, 'No. No.'

So here it was. I'd kind of known it for weeks. Had scribbled in my notebook several times: 'Cecily – affair?' And now it was out in the open. Well, kind of. It felt a relief. Perhaps now the work could start and we could all stop shilly-shallying around. It wasn't that Cecily had told me in words, it was just that everything she said about herself and their life together screamed AFFAIR! AFFAIR! AFFAIR! What was interesting was why Kamal had taken so very long to cotton on. Or even to ask the question why she always seemed to have to work late and why she was constantly needing to make phone calls at the weekend. Was this a deliberate turning of a blind eye, I wondered? Did Kamal actively not want to know? Or perhaps this failure to notice was something more deeply unconscious?

They'd been coming for several months at Cecily's instigation. She said she was worried that things had got a bit stale between them and that if they didn't do something, they'd end up like their parents. Cecily's hair was startlingly short, cropped close to her head and bleached blonde; one nostril was pierced with a tiny diamond and she was petite and deliciously rounded. She reminded me of Rihanna and had the same glow and sensuality as the singer, though in reality she was nothing so glamorous as she had recently been elected as a local politician in the far reaches of east London. Kamal was also striking. He was always dressed in black and his hair, long and straight, was just beginning to be streaked with grey and he wore it tied back into a low bun. There was something cool and clever about them – and they were a bit cool in their approach to the therapy, too.

At the first session, Kamal seemed barely interested in me or the process and when I asked them why they'd come, he said it was for Cecily; he thought they were fine and didn't really believe in talking to a stranger about their relationship. Then he grilled me about my experience, my qualifications and my fee. Could they negotiate to pay less? Could they have a reduction because they had three children? I enquired about their financial situation; I didn't want to be rigid if they really couldn't afford it but it became quickly clear that both had reasonable earnings, so, instead, I turned my attention to his ambivalence about coming. I didn't get far. Kamal was abrupt and stuck to his guns that he was here because she'd asked him to come, and if Cecily wanted that, he supposed he would go along with it.

Twenty minutes in and Kamal's hostility had melted away, to be replaced by a charming but somewhat cool front. It soon became clear that the ambivalence about coming for therapy was in fact shared by both of them. It took ages to agree a session time because Cecily was so busy. She asked if I could see them at 7am. Or perhaps I worked at 10pm? Were Saturday mornings or Sunday afternoons possible? It was clear that it was going to be tough for them to make a commitment to couple therapy.

When, several weeks later, they did eventually start their sessions, it seemed they didn't know what to talk about. Kamal would often be quiet and only interested in hearing what Cecily had to say. When she did speak, it was in a roundabout, unspecific way about how unhappy she was. A kind of impatience would come over me about wasting so much time; this prevarication and evasion was frustrating. His slightly superior nonchalance and her trippy vagueness made it harder for me to see this as a defence and that underneath, they were most probably very frightened of what might happen if they really began to talk.

The unhappiness seemed to stem from Kamal's disinterest in having sex but this was skirted around, mentioned only in passing or jest, so we never could explore it in any depth. In some sessions, they talked, in a stilted manner, about their children, who were four, three and two, but even these conversations never seemed to develop. What things I said felt rather dull and pedestrian, as though I'd taken my comments from some rather basic 'Making Your Marriage Work' handbook. They wouldn't let me in and so I had nothing meaningful to say.

The weeks went by and all I heard was more and more about Cecily's busyness. Kamal would pick the children up from nursery. Kamal would make the children their tea. Kamal would put them to bed and then Cecily would come home, often slightly drunk, and wake them up to cuddle. I was, in truth, feeling more and more judgemental about her. But still Kamal seemed dead set on avoiding any showdown. He would only say mildly that he thought Billy, their four-year-old, would like to see more of her. And then I would hear that Kamal had spent the weekend on his own with the children and Cecily had gone to a conference for work.

She eventually told him about the affair in the session just before the Easter break. It came out because he wanted her to go to his parents in Turkey for the holidays and she'd been resisting. 'I have to work; you know I have to work. I'll need to spend the bank holiday canvassing; I can't be out of the country for the whole week. *You* take the kids and I'll fly over after the Easter weekend, if I can.' This statement sat in the room like a stark challenge. Kamal had said the previous week how much he was looking forward to spending time with her and she'd promised that she'd put the children first – but here she was backtracking. I found myself feeling very cross with her; it seemed so provocative.

Kamal looked defeated. Then he rallied, turned his head to look at her and said, 'Are you lying to me, Cecily? Don't lie to me.' She looked at him, panicked. Then she looked at me.

'I think he wants you to be straight with him, Cecily.' I knew, as I spoke, that she knew I knew.

She nodded. A look of terror spread across her face. 'I'm really sorry.' And, after a long pause, 'You know, don't you? You know I've been seeing someone else?'

Kamal put his head between his hands. It looked like he was trying to shut out what she was saying. Cecily was agitated and crying, 'I'm sorry . . . I'm so sorry.'

I watched, silent and transfixed.

'Who?' asked Kamal, his voice hard and angry.

There was a silence and then, in a small, quiet voice, she said, 'Frankie.' And then he erupted.

Kamal's explosion and anger was like a passing cloud; by the next session, he seemed almost back to his cool, calm and in control self. But as they began to talk, for once they let me in and showed me how things really were. They'd talked exhaustively since they'd left the previous week, staying up into the small hours, riding these big, emotional waves, taking it in turns to weep in despair. Every single night they'd conclude they had to separate and then, every morning, they'd wake at dawn and, desperate and broken, they'd make love and be back at square one. Because they were now completely open to each other, I had a sense that they were more connected than they'd ever been.

From experience, I know that an affair can sometimes be a catalyst towards something much more satisfying, particularly when a relationship has avoided all conflict, leading to something stultifying and dead. In conflict-free relationships, there is often no sex at all but the discovery of an affair can trigger desire and suddenly there is passionate love-making. Why might this be so? One part of the reason is with the truth now on the table, all certainty about the future is gone and love-making becomes a way for the couple to mutually reassure each other, re-establishing the illusion of some sense of security. But I've also noticed that an affair can make a couple see each other differently; being suddenly separate and wanted by someone else can bring new excitement and desire. Was Cecily's affair going to shake something up between them that would bring them closer or was her affair a transitional process that would lead her out of the relationship towards a real separation? Was it *in*fidelity or *out*fidelity?

'It's not serious, Kam. You don't have to be threatened by Frankie,' Cecily pleaded. 'You know I just needed to find out what it'd be like, being with a woman.' And then it dawned on me that Frankie wasn't a man.

'But Frankie, of all people? I don't understand how you could do that. Don't you know the first principle? Don't shit in your own backyard.'

It became clear that they were both close and intimate friends with Frankie. She was politically active and a comrade of Cecily's, and she lived just around the corner and had children the same age as theirs. Her husband had left the previous year and since then, she'd been in their life on a daily basis. Kam took Frankie's kids to nursery; Frankie picked up theirs. Kam had Frankie's kids for sleepovers when she wanted to go out . . . out, it now transpired, with Cecily. Whilst Kam had been caring for the children, Frankie and Cecily were around the corner making love.

As this story unfolded, I wondered how Kamal could be so calm. It was *such* a betrayal, so humiliating to do this with someone so central to their lives. I felt the outrage boil inside me whilst Kam, still impassive, refused to. As the session drew to a close, Kam said that Cecily should have a session on her own with me – she needed help to decide what she wanted to do. He was going to Istanbul as planned and the kids were coming with him.

Cecily looked pinched and thin as she sat down the following week, her plump glow gone. She rummaged in her bag, apologised for nothing in particular and then, with her own tissues safely positioned on her lap, she burst into tears.

'What shall I do? What shall I do, Susanna? I'm going to fuck up Kam, fuck up the kids, fuck up our home. What shall I do?' She blew her nose loudly and looked at me as though I could give her an answer. 'I love Kam. I love our life together. I don't know why I've done this. I've tried and tried to break it off with Frankie but . . .' She trailed off. 'Tell me what to do. Please.'

'It's really hard to be in such a dilemma. I can see how torn you feel,' I said neutrally.

She took a deep breath. Looked at me. Then looked away.

'Will I fuck up the kids?'

'If you leave?' I asked.

She nodded. 'I don't want what *I* want to hurt them . . . how can I justify that?'

'It sounds as though you feel it's either them or you? Is it quite that stark?'

'Kamal will hate me. The kids will hate me . . .'

'I think you're frightened of how much you might hate yourself?'

'Yes. I do hate myself and I'm going to hate myself either way.' And she began to cry again.

As the session went on, Cecily told me more about her relationship with Frankie and how it had been a revelation for them both. Neither had been with a woman before. She felt that they really got each other – partly because they were both women and like her Frankie was mixed race and very politically engaged. They were deeply in love and as she spoke to me, she conveyed the intensity and pleasure of their physical relationship.

'I've also loved being with Kam but I'm not sure he's loved being with me.'

'Sexually, you mean?'

'Yeah.' She paused. 'It's never been that great. He's never seemed keen. I mean, even this last couple of weeks we've had a lot of sex but, well, it's all my initiative, not his.'

'I think you feel really desired by Frankie and really *not* desired by Kam.'

'Exactly. Yes, exactly. She *wants* me. I don't think he does. Not really. I don't think he ever has. And since I was elected, it's hard for us to share stuff. Frankie knows what I'm doing and why. I don't think Kam really gets it.'

We sat in silence.

'He can't come,' she said suddenly. 'He doesn't come. I've never been able to make him come. It's gone on for years.'

I waited, wondering about the children and how they'd

been 'made'. As though following my thoughts, Cecily said, 'We went to a clinic. In Oxford. We had IUI.'

'IUI?'

'I forget what it stands for but basically he masturbated into a jar and then they injected me. They checked when I was fertile. Worked every time, straight away.'

Lots of questions went through my head. How had they decided this? Why hadn't they sought treatment for this difficulty and why had she gone along with it? And why, if the sex had always been that problematic, had she got involved with him in the first place?

'It sounds as though things haven't been satisfactory for either of you.'

She shrugged. 'I don't know. I don't think Kam ever minded.'

I was left puzzled and surprised. I'd known that Kamal was less keen on having sex than her but he was devoted to Cecily. His whole identity conveyed his wish to be a good husband and father and he emanated a very masculine confidence. It was hard to put that persona together with what Cecily had just told me.

There were no seats on the crowded Tube. From Euston to Camden Town, I hung from the strap and hoped someone would give up their seat. Just as I was beginning to accept that I'd be standing all the way to Highgate, a tall man in his thirties smiled at me, gesturing to ask if I wanted to sit. I nodded gratefully and swapped places with him, plonking myself down on the warm moquette. This gallant deed took my thoughts back to Kamal. Clearly there was something important going on surrounding sexual identity. It wasn't the first time that I'd come across a situation like this. If Cecily now thought she was probably lesbian and Kam didn't seem to like sex with her, what did this mean? Had there been an unconscious collusion between them that had largely kept sex off the agenda? Were both in fact unsure about their hetero-sexuality and was that why they'd – unconsciously – chosen each other?

Understanding and working with sexuality can be the most puzzling part of my job and I've long wondered why that might be. Part of the reason is of course the difficulty that many couples have in sharing the very intimate details of their lives, but it's also because sexual desire, and the fantasies that inevitably accompany it, are often buried in the deeper layers of the unconscious, hard to reach and disconnected from words and reason. Couples quite often come with a sex-ual 'symptom' – bringing difficulties that prevent them from having a satisfying sex life together. Whilst some of these sex-ual 'symptoms' can be relatively straightforward, sometimes they are not. Strong, potent husbands are disgusted by their wives' bodies but excited by elder porn; loving, open and friendly wives are unable to be aroused and remain frozen and unmoved when touched. Our bodies tell the story but translating the story into something verbal, which can be understood and shared, can be very difficult to do.

Because of the Easter holidays, it was nearly three weeks before I saw either of them again. There had been some back and forth on email and we'd agreed that Kam would also have a session on his own. It was a beautiful spring day and I popped out to take a short walk in the afternoon sun. As I approached my office, I could see Kam on his phone, deep in conversation just outside the building. He was wearing a col-ourful, embroidered scarf and looked tanned and healthy as he stood in the sun. He didn't look broken or distressed but, rather, flourishing.

Fifteen minutes later, this brown, handsome man took a seat on my couch, his mobile clutched in his hand.

'Sorry, but I need to keep this on,' he said, gesturing to his iPhone. 'Urgent stuff at work, I'm afraid.' I nodded and noted to myself how casual and cool he seemed, how distant.

'When did we last see you? Seems ages.' He blew out his cheeks.

He then chattered on about his visit to Istanbul and how much the children had loved seeing their grandparents. He talked about how Cecily didn't really understand his obligations to his family and he guessed these were cultural differences that they hadn't properly talked about and really should. He talked about the children being mixed race and how his parents were upset that they weren't bringing them up as good Muslims. These were important things that we hadn't discussed before but his tone was dismissive and superficial, so that I began to have the distinct feeling I was being shut out. He made me feel foolish for being worried about them, as though he was completely fine and there was nothing he or they needed from me now. I observed him constructing this persona and knew this coolness was, most likely, a reaction to the break in the therapy and his way of dealing with it, so I waited, open to what might happen next.

Eventually, he fell silent, as if he knew that he was wasting his time. The sun, now low in the sky, was in my eyes and, as I squinted at him through the brightness, I saw his face had fallen and suddenly he looked weary and sad.

'I think it must be very difficult for you, Kam, to be in this situation. I know it's important to you to feel as though you've got everything sorted. I know you don't like to feel like you're someone who's in a mess, who needs help.'

He smiled at me warmly, his beautiful brown eyes crinkling in what seemed like amusement at my comment. 'Maybe. You might have a point. But I'm sure you can understand that I've got to hold it together right now. Cecily's in a state, so I've got to deal with that, right? And my main concern is the children. It's them who'll suffer. Right? I need to be there for them, right?'

I said nothing. He was looking for confirmation and I couldn't give it to him.

'Cecily's broken it off. With Frankie. And we're moving. I've put our house on the market. We've agreed it's best if we get some distance . . . From Frankie,' he explained, noting the slightly questioning look on my face.

I didn't know what to say. Was this plan of action, which seemed full of certainty, Kam's way of dealing with something that was actually very uncertain? Was Cecily sure about this? Was Kam? But I sensed that if I challenged him directly, he'd simply push back.

'It sounds as though you've both made some serious decisions since I last saw you. I think you want me to see that everything's now sorted and settled.'

There was a moment's hesitation during which I felt he was weighing up whether to continue with this false front or whether to let me in. Eventually he scoffed 'Settled?' and looked at me as though I'd said something very stupid. 'No, it's not "settled". Every day it changes. It's actually driving me mad. One minute, Cecily's at home, putting the kids to bed, reading stories, being Mrs Mummy and then – boom! She disappears and we don't see her for . . .' He trailed off.

'It must be hard, Kam, very hard for you. It must make it hard to work out what *you* want?'

He nodded and we were silent for a bit.

'She told you, didn't she.' It wasn't a question, so I waited. 'I was cross with her. I didn't think you needed to know.' I felt puzzled. Was he talking about the affair or about his sexual difficulties? I tipped my head to one side, an uncertain look on my face. 'About the children. How they were conceived,' he clarified.

I nodded. 'Yes, she told me about that.'

He fell silent again.

'Perhaps it feels too painful to talk about?'

He looked at me piercingly, as though deciding, once more, whether he could trust me. There was a heartbeat of hesitation, and then he began to talk. He told me he'd never had any real problems before he met Cecily; he'd had many girlfriends and many one-night stands where sex had been usually fine. But with Cecily, it was different. He'd never really cared about anyone before he met her; none of his relationships lasted more than a few months and, if he was being honest with me, he didn't think he'd been a great boyfriend. He'd never been faithful. He'd done a lot of travelling, worked in the Far East and he hadn't ever wanted to get serious with anyone. Then he met Cecily. He'd just got back from a stint working in Beijing, where he'd been very lonely. When they met, she wasn't in a good way. She was smoking a lot of dope and she'd just split up with a guy who'd treated her badly. Then, a couple of months after they got together, her mother got cancer and died. It had made them incredibly close. I asked him gently if it was then the problem with sex began?

'Maybe, well, yes. I don't know why. But yes. It was about then. When her mother got sick. It was very stressful.'

'Maybe it felt like you were there to protect Cecily, to look after her, rather than to take anything for yourself, including your own pleasure?'

'Well, that's kind of how it's always been. I don't mind though,' he reassured me quickly.

'Don't you?' I asked. 'I think perhaps you do. And maybe your reluctance to have sex is one way you've been "complaining" about how uneven and perhaps unfair things feel between you?'

He looked thoughtful. We were over time and it felt hard

to tell him we had to stop as it felt as if the session was just beginning. He got up swiftly, pasted a smile on his face and left my office without a backward glance. I could hear him running down the stairs, purposefully taking two or three steps at a time.

I opened my laptop to check my email but something was tugging at my mind. When I applied in 1986 to become a marriage guidance counsellor, I was asked what I thought my biggest challenge would be. It wasn't difficult to answer – I was fresh from a passionate engagement with feminism and had spent years marching for women's rights, attending conferences and consciousness raising groups. I was, I told the selection committee, worried that I wouldn't be able to cope with the men: the bullying husbands demanding sex and pushing around their wives. But, for whatever reason, these men have been almost entirely absent from my consulting room. Instead, for most of my career, it's tended towards the opposite – angry, accusing women and rather compliant but disconnected and withdrawn men. And here we were again with what seemed like a very clear power differential. Kam, so easy-going and cool, seemed to give way to Cecily, who was demanding and hot. But was it really quite like that?

How power is expressed between a couple seems to me to be central to how a couple's sex life fares. Where a couple can each allow domains of authority, where each has 'influencing' power within the relationship, sex is often just another arena to play with these issues. Ideally, the 'leadership' moves around, each partner taking it in turns to take up the reins. Via this dance, a kind of equality of arms is reached, where what is most valued by the couple is the creative exchange that brings forth new thoughts, ideas, projects and sexual pleasures. Problems seem to arise in a couple's sex life when the relationship has stopped developing and has become rigid and inflexible. In these marriages, the roles each partner takes become fixed and the natural ebb and flow of give and take, power and vulnerability, strength and weakness is lost.

When Cecily and Kam arrived the following week, they seemed even more subdued than usual. Cecily was full of a cold, tissues in hand, and even Kam looked less burnished than usual. They looked at each other.

'You start,' said Cecily.

And he did. He started by explaining how low Cecily was. How hard things were for her. Until I interrupted and pointed out he was talking about her feelings and not his own.

'He always does that,' said Cecily. 'He never talks about himself. He's never down. He's never cross. You're like a bloody robot, Kam. Even now, even now with this going on, you're like nothing's wrong. Like things are just normal!' Her voice was wobbly with pain and frustration.

'I don't know what you want me to say, Cecily. Not everything needs to be a big drama – I'm not like you. I don't burst into tears or behave like a child when I don't get what I want, but I'm definitely not OK. I'm not fucking OK. Right? Right?'

Cecily's eyes flared open in alarm – but here it was, the frustration and anger that Kam tried so hard to control. I was beginning to understand more about what was going on between them. The way that Cecily expressed the frustration for *both* of them. The ways she held all the ugly, selfish, needy feelings for *both* of them. He'd disavowed these parts of himself, become the all-good hero giver, whilst she scrabbled around in the muck of feelings and conflicts, being selfish and feeling guilt about that selfishness.

They glared at each other and, for the first time, I could see hatred in their eyes.

'I think you both feel stuck. Stuck with ugly feelings and

guilty feelings about that ugliness. And a fear that if you choose to separate, you'll never recover, and the children will never recover.'

They looked stricken and tearful – the hatred evaporated. How quickly their feelings could change.

'I don't want to hurt you, Kam.'

'I know. I know.'

I could feel their sadness; there was a truth in it. There was silence for a beat and then the sadness evaporated and the toxic hatred was back.

'Maybe you should see someone. You've obviously got a problem,' Kam spat.

'You think being lesbian is a problem? Christ, Kam, you sound like your stupid, ignorant mother . . .' Cecily scoffed.

'How difficult it is to stay with the sadness,' I pointed out.

Kam looked at me. 'Will the children be badly affected? I only care about them now.'

'It depends how you separate. It depends how you work things out once you are separated.'

And I talked about the research and how children can recover from divorce but that the kind of relationship parents have, even when separated, has a big impact. If they collaborated, if they avoided conflict and blaming, the children could probably manage it. And I also talked about how staying together wouldn't necessarily be better if they were deeply unhappy and angry with each other.

A week later, Kam came on his own as we'd agreed that it might be better if they had some sessions just for themselves. As he walked into my room, he handed me a hessian bag printed with a red cockerel on the front.

'For you' he gestured with his head as he struggled out of his jacket.

I looked at him enquiringly and placed the bag on the floor by the door.

'Rainier cherries – the best. We import them. They just came in today. The season's *verrry* short. Three weeks, maybe.'

I smiled.

'I wanted to say thank you. I think we're in a much better place and I think we know we're going to separate.' He paused. 'It's OK. We're going to come next week together – we want to discuss what to say to the children. Hope that's OK?'

'Of course.'

'I wanted to talk about my . . . er . . . difficulty. You know. With sex.'

I nodded. And as I looked down, I could see the hessian bag and the image of the red cockerel out of the corner of my eye and it occurred to me, here was such a clear symbol of male potency.

'You said in that session when I came on my own that you thought my problem was because I was angry with Cecily?'

I nodded.

'I'm not sure that's right.' There was a long pause and I waited for Kam to say more.

'When I was about 15, my mother caught me looking at porn.' He looked around the room, as though trying to find an escape route.

Hesitantly, he told me what porn he'd been watching and, though he struggled to be explicit, I gradually came to understand that it was incestuous in nature and involved a boy and his younger sister. His mother had been furious and had told him he was sick and a pervert. He felt as though his mother had never quite looked at him the same after that. We talked about how ashamed he'd felt and he wondered if that experience had made him 'funny' about sex. He certainly often felt guilty about it. Guilty if he didn't try to have sex with Cecily and very guilty when they did.

'You've never talked to me about your sister, Kam,' I said, sometime later.

'No. We don't get on. She's gone back to Istanbul and lives near my parents. I don't really see her, even when we visit.'

Jasmina, he told me, was a year younger than him and had always been the 'weakling' of the family and used that to manipulate his parents. She was always complaining and a real pain but his parents worshipped the ground she walked on.

'Did you have to look after her when you were children?' I asked.

'Not really. My mother wouldn't have trusted me, I was too mean to her. I was always in trouble for not being nice enough to her or for hitting her or taking her toys.' He laughed. 'She had my parents wrapped round her little finger . . . still does.'

'You felt she was the favourite? That they preferred her to you?'

'Abso-fucking-lutely! My mother was always telling me to be more like her and to be nice to her.'

Then he said, shamefaced, 'The porn . . . it wasn't about her. The girl in it wasn't anything like Jasmina.'

We were silent for a while, both of us contemplating this link. Then I said, 'I think, Kam, there are lots of things wrapped up in this "symptom" of yours. There are the mixed feelings you have about Cecily, about having to give way to her needs a lot – perhaps like you were expected to do with your sister. And there are the mixed feelings of loving Cecily and your sister but at times hating them too?'

He nodded. 'Cecily and my sister have quite a lot in common. Not looks-wise, but in some ways they're both very . . .' he searched for the words, '. . . difficult but also fragile.'

'Perhaps, when you've felt sexual towards Cecily – who you believe is fragile – a part of you hasn't been sure whether your sexual feelings are loving or destructive? Whether your penis is a good thing or something rather bad. And you bring me cherries in a bag with a big cock on it.' I said, smiling.

He laughed and then he looked at me intently. 'I think my mother thought sex was just a bad thing. And especially a bad thing for a woman.'

'Well, that's a powerful message you got from your mother. When you don't come inside Cecily, are you protecting her? But maybe you're punishingly withholding something from her, too?'

I'd like to tell you that after these sessions everything got sorted. But psychotherapy isn't like that. For every step forward, there are often steps back. Therapy progresses in a spiral, looping back and forth, reworking old conflicts and circling around new challenges. Jung described it well: 'We can hardly escape the feeling that the unconscious process moves spiral-wise round a centre, gradually getting closer, while the characteristics of the centre grow more and more distinct.'*

Cecily and Kam continued in therapy for another six months before Cecily moved out to live with Frankie. During those months, they cried a lot but they also became gradually gentler with each other and more determined to work together to ensure the children were protected as much as possible. In the last sessions, when they came alone, I sensed they both felt relieved it was over. Cecily seemed more grounded and happier, and Kam, slightly nervously, told me he had begun seeing a woman he worked with, someone much younger than him.

* Carl Jung, *Collected Works of C.G. Jung* (Routledge, 1973).

During those six months, I was never quite sure what the outcome would be. Would they find a way to stay together or would they split? When couples skirt that border between separation and staying together it always feels utterly mysterious to me. I never know when someone will cross that border from being *in* the relationship, however disappointing, to standing on the other side, out of it. For me, it's even more mysterious than the process of falling in love and becoming a couple. Sometimes, couples come right up against the separation and then pull back and this can be because a psychic separation has taken place, rather than an actual house move – each partner becoming more their own person and less entangled with each other. Sometimes, couples don't properly separate at all. Each moves to a new home, they get new partners, even have more children, but they can never quite let each other go.

RHODA FEEDS ON THE POISON APPLE

I'd just returned from the Easter break when this email appeared in my inbox:

> *Dear Susanna,*
>
> *My daughter tells me I need a shrink. I found your name online. How much do you charge for a session?*
>
> *Regards,*
> *Rhoda*

I wrote back:

> *Dear Rhoda,*
>
> *Thank you for your enquiry. We could meet for a consultation at my practice in Queen Anne Street next Wednesday at 10.15. Would that suit?*
> *My fee would be £XX.*
>
> *Best wishes,*
> *Susanna*

An hour later, I received a reply:

> *I'll think about it.*

Whilst it's not unusual for an enquiry to evaporate without outcome, it is unusual for a prospective patient to be so forthright about their ambivalence. It was rather refreshing, to be honest. I remember years ago, a senior colleague saying that one would always find the most ambivalence about starting therapy right at the moment someone makes the first contact. In the various clinics I've worked in, it was expected that at least a third of the enquiries we received wouldn't progress to any treatment.

However, a few days later the following email arrived in my inbox:

> *I've thought about it.*
> *I'll come on Wednesday at 10.15am as you requested.*
> *Please let me have your bank details so I can pay you the required amount. However, I must say your fee seems very expensive to me.*
>
> *Regards,*
> *Rhoda*

Given the brusque nature of this communication, it was with some trepidation (and curiosity) that on Wednesday morning I awaited Rhoda's arrival. I smiled as I opened my door and gestured for her to come in, as she seemed to hesitate on the threshold. She did not smile back.

'Where do you want me?' she asked. 'Shall I lie down there?' She pointed at my sofa.

'Why don't you just take a seat today,' I suggested, and with that she perched rather awkwardly on the edge of the chair and screwed up her eyes to scrutinise me as closely as possible. She was a petite woman, elegant and athletic, with cropped short, silver hair. Her hands, which she folded in her lap, looked strong and purposeful.

She then launched into what felt like a prepared speech in which she proceeded to tell me, in no uncertain terms, that she thought it highly unlikely I'd be able to help her. She was only here because her daughter, Tamar, had thought it a good idea. She mentioned several times that I was expensive and even at one point asked directly why I charged so much. I told her this was my usual fee but that if she was struggling financially this could be discussed. She waved a hand dismissively and eventually managed to tell me what had brought her to my consulting room. Her concerns centred on her childhood friend Michelle, whom she was no longer in contact with. They'd known each other since they were babes in arms as their mothers had been close friends. It seemed, from what she relayed, that she and Michelle had been inseparable most of their lives. However, they'd fallen out and Rhoda had 'cut' Michelle from her life. When I commented that this must have been extremely sad after such a long friendship, Rhoda scoffed disdainfully.

As the session progressed and I dug a little deeper, Rhoda described how Michelle had committed an unforgivable betrayal. But as she spoke about the events that had led to their estrangement, she became increasingly animated and less and less coherent.

'I've never spoken to anyone in *my life* the way *she* spoke to me. It was just rude, really rude and . . .' she fished around for the right word. 'Rude!'

I couldn't help thinking how ironic it was that the word she used to describe Michelle was just the word that I'd been thinking fitted her.

Rhoda's narrative was long and winding but, eventually, I began to get a clearer picture of what had happened between them. It seemed that although Michelle had been Rhoda's closest friend and confidante, they'd often had ups and downs. Over the years, they'd fallen out over a broken vase, over a holiday booked and then cancelled and hadn't spoken for a year because Rhoda had taken exception to Michelle's new dog. But when Rhoda's husband had left her, Michelle and Rhoda had renewed their bond and they had become very friendly and close.

'It sounds like Michelle is the one you turned to when things got really tough,' I suggested gently.

'Not really,' Rhoda bristled, 'we just hung out together. She was single. I was suddenly on my own – it was . . . convenient. And it wasn't "really tough", either. My husband was an idiot and when he left, it was, frankly, rather marvellous.'

I didn't know quite how to reply to that but I noted the angry scorn in her voice and the way she'd pushed back very strongly at my attempt to connect with a softer side of her.

'The problem with Michelle, as I've been trying to explain to you, is that she's rather conventional, terribly finicky – judgemental,' Rhoda concluded and I gave her a quizzical look to encourage her to continue. 'She didn't approve of Nigel.'

'Nigel?'

'When I started to see Nigel, she thought it was . . .' she shrugged her shoulders. 'Wrong. She doesn't approve of affairs.' Rhoda rolled her eyes and sat back, waiting for me to speak.

'And that's why you stopped speaking to her?'

She then explained that Michelle had avoided asking her to dinner. Michelle made a big Friday night dinner every week and Rhoda had gone regularly but now suddenly she was '*persona non grata*'.

'She made her feelings crystal clear. She may not have said anything directly but I'm not stupid – she treated me like a pariah and she treated Nigel worse.'

'Did you talk to her about it?' I asked. She looked at me

contemptuously, as though my question was ridiculous, and then, ignoring my enquiry, she continued with her story.

'Every year, we all go to my house on the Isle of Wight. Michelle and her family, my children. We've been doing it for years. Then, because Nigel was coming, *she* didn't want to come. And then because *she* wasn't coming her children didn't either.'

'She didn't come because she doesn't like Nigel?' I asked, trying to get the story straight.

'No! She doesn't *approve*. Because he was well, sort of married. He doesn't really even live with his wife, most of the time, so I don't know why she made such a silly fuss about it.'

She went on to explain that, as far as she was concerned, Michelle's behaviour was completely unacceptable, so she'd told Michelle their friendship was over. I asked Rhoda how Michelle had taken this and Rhoda, scornfully, said that Michelle had cried and made a huge fuss.

'But she's a bit of a drama queen anyway, so she's always making a fuss about something or other. She sends me a birthday card every year with some stupid sentimental message in it. I don't know why she bothers. It's a ridiculous waste of time and money. She can't seem to get it through her head that we're no longer friends.'

The 'every year' snagged and I began to wonder how long it was since this falling-out had taken place.

'How long ago did this happen, Rhoda?' I asked.

'Ten, maybe eleven years. I can't really remember.'

'Oh!' I exclaimed, failing to hide my surprise. 'Well, that's quite a long while. It makes me wonder why you're coming now. Why does your daughter think you need to come now?'

'She thinks I'm obsessed.'

'Obsessed with Michelle? Are you?' I asked.

She didn't answer my question but proceeded to show me the answer by talking for the next 20 minutes about Michelle and the various unforgivable things she'd done. She felt betrayed and wronged and also angry that Michelle had 'got away with it'. Her daughter was also in the firing line because she remained close with Michelle's children and had continued to celebrate birthdays and Christmases in her presence.

'My daughter wants me to "make it up" with Michelle so she can invite her to the wedding.'

'The wedding?'

'Tamar's getting married at Christmas,' she replied curtly, as though I was somehow slow for not knowing her daughter was getting married.

Betrayal comes in many forms; it occurs between lovers, between colleagues and between siblings. But betrayal between women friends seems to be particularly disillusioning and hard to recover from. Over the years, I've observed the nature of women's relationships and the particular quality of those bonds. As women mature and give up the fantasy of the ideal lover – the selfless heroic prince who'll care for them seamlessly and selflessly – and as they face the fact that their lover isn't and cannot be a good mother to them, they often seem to compensate for this by turning to their friends for that particular kind of unquestioning, unconditional care. Frequently, friendships between women are constructed to confirm each other by mirroring and harmonising, protecting each other from harsh reality. In these reassuring and like-minded states, female friendship tries to recover the romantic ideal, providing a cosy bubble away from disappointments and limitations. But friendship can be hard to maintain, jealousies can emerge when one friend has more than the other and when that bubble bursts, a vengeful fury can be unleashed, the unspoken contract not to question, disapprove or challenge lies in tatters and visceral hatred replaces the romance.

I once had a patient, many, many years ago, who purported to be a witch; she celebrated the solstice, kept many cats and always wore black. She earned her living making penis- and vagina-shaped candles but she also wrote personalised spells and incantations that she sold on the internet. Mostly her customers were other women and in one session she gave me a series of printed cards with curses printed on them.

By the witch's breath
And the darkening storm
I invoke my anger
And wish you grievous harm

Since your sight is flawed
And your heart unkind
I invoke my anger
To turn your green eyes blind

When the dawn is breaking
And the light comes back
I won't need my anger
I won't feel the lack

But you, my dear, will suffer
In your crazy mind
From envy, fear and darkness
From guilt that chafes and binds.

I saw Rhoda for a dozen sessions before she decided my services were no longer required. She sought from me an audience for her grudge, not a solution or a route to healing.

I worked hard to encourage her to explore why she was so preoccupied. Could we make, perhaps, a link to some loss or sense of betrayal in her past? Was there some unfinished business that this falling-out with Michelle had come to symbolise for her? But I got nowhere; she loved her anger and enjoyed sharing her grievance with me. It was as though she couldn't see the poison inside the shiny red apple of revenge.

As I struggled to help her move on, I came to see that her sense of betrayal had become an integral part of who she was. To lose or lessen this grievance, to change her feelings towards Michelle in any way, would have meant confronting and grieving her loss; something she was too afraid to do. Every year that she'd wasted on the grudge had to be justified so that the anger and bitterness she felt towards Michelle was required to grow, year in, year out. All this hatred provided the oxygen to justify her position and I felt that in her unrelenting refusal to mourn and forgive she was trying to destroy her need for love.

After weeks of listening to her bitter complaints, I began to think of Rhoda as a kind of Miss Havisham, the scorned and bitter spinster of Dickens's novel *Great Expectations,* who, betrayed by her lover, turns forever away from life. Miss Havisham is envious and withholding, training her young ward, Estella, to hate men and to break their hearts, killing her capacity for love. 'But that, in shutting out the light of day, she had shut out infinitely more; that, in seclusion, she had secluded herself from a thousand natural healing influences; that, her mind, brooding solitary, had grown diseased . . .'

I thought that Rhoda was also filled with envy and, like the evil queen in Snow White, she was both poisoned and poisonous in her vengeance.

I'd come across this kind of difficulty before and recognised the bleakness of its tenacious hold on some patients. It was an addiction to a kind of psychic revenge, one that was crushing her much more than it was affecting the object of her hate. I pointed out that her vindictive feelings seemed to be taking her nowhere, that Michelle's attempts to reconnect sounded loving and hopeful, whilst she seemed to be suffering terribly. Her anger had become a kind of poison infecting her whole life and now she was in danger of seriously falling out with her daughter. I tried to help her to see that revenge is pointless if the act is masochistic.

'Rhoda, it's almost as if you don't care if you hurt yourself, as long as you can hold onto the fantasy that you're getting back at Michelle. It's as if you're driving your brand new BMW into her garden wall each day – her wall might have lost a brick or two but you keep totalling your brand new car.'

But nothing I said seemed to move Rhoda. She remained untouched and unreachable and ended her treatment without, it seemed, a backward glance.

DON JUAN GROWS UP AND SETTLES DOWN

James was a rather unprepossessing patient considering his reputation as a Lothario. He contacted me by text in late July saying he'd read something I'd written in a newspaper article about infidelity that had struck him enormously and did I by any chance have an appointment I could offer? I replied that I didn't currently but thought it likely I'd have a space when I returned from holiday in September. 'Could you wait?' I asked. The answer came back immediately that he'd be only too happy to wait and that he was really looking forward to meeting me.

I love holidays and many psychotherapists plan their breaks to coincide with the academic year. The period up to the long summer vacation, however, can be wearying for psychotherapists. There's the natural tiredness everyone feels at the end of a long year but it can also be tough because it's common for long-term patients to end their treatment just before the August break. Thus, alongside the build-up of excitement and anticipation at the thought of a month to myself, there's often a tinge of sadness at bringing to a close sessions with patients who've been on a long journey with me.

It's common knowledge that psychotherapists get their largest number of referrals at two points in the year: in September, after the summer holidays, and in January, after the Christmas holidays. This particular September was no different; my email and phone were full of messages from potential patients wanting appointments and there were several friendly prompts from James, reminding me I'd 'committed' to seeing him on my return.

James's texts led me to expect a dynamic and engaging person but when he entered my consulting room, he seemed rather nondescript – someone you'd walk past in the street without a second glance. His hair appeared unwashed and thinning, his clothes were ill-fitting and his trainers were caked with the dirt of ages. He seemed bowed and rather fragile.

He told me he'd wanted to come because, at an after-work drinks party, his friend had described him as 'a bigger philanderer than Boris Johnson'. Everyone laughed but whilst the all-male group seemed good-natured and jocular about this description, James felt deeply uncomfortable. He'd gone home that evening 'feeling really sick', been unable to sleep that night and this nausea and sleep disturbance had continued from then on. He spoke at length about how previously he'd been a very good sleeper and generally untroubled about things but since that evening, he really hadn't been able to settle down to anything.

I tried to explore with James what he'd found so troubling about the off-hand remark. Was it the actual idea of himself as a philanderer? Indeed, did he think it to be true? Or perhaps he'd felt humiliated in some way?

He listened to me carefully but seemed unable to pinpoint what had distressed him so much or whether the flippant Boris comparison had any basis in truth. 'I just don't get any of it. Usually, I sail through stuff but something about this has really got to me.' He then gave me a big smile and added, 'I'm hoping you'll be able to tell me why.'

There are multiple reasons why people have affairs but, in my experience, it is often to do with something that is going on between the couple. An affair can be a response to a problem the couple aren't able to deal with together and sometimes the betrayal acts as a useful red flag. On the other hand, an affair can be a response to the lessening of attachment to a partner and a transition out of the relationship towards something new. But, in this instance, it seemed that James's continual infidelity probably wasn't much to do with his girlfriend but rather spoke to something about James and his difficulties with intimate relationships more generally.

The rest of the session seemed to proceed at a snail's pace; it was stilted and at times had a rather excruciating awkwardness to it. What I suggested to him didn't seem to connect and my silence seemed to make him agitated. As we came to the end, I discussed the fee I would charge, the time I could offer on a regular basis and other administrative details of beginning therapy. I said that it seemed that it had been difficult for us to get to the bottom of what feelings were keeping him awake at night but perhaps we might meet again for a further consultation and think a bit more about it all? Immediately he came to life, saying firmly that yes, he definitely wanted to come back and that all the arrangements were fine and he would see me next week.

After he left, I remember feeling an initial uncertainty about whether I really wanted to see him again. I harboured serious doubts that he'd be able to settle down to treatment and I wondered if he and I made a good 'fit'. But, although James certainly hadn't made my heart sing with anticipation during our first session, this made me curious about the reason why. On the phone and in text, he'd seemed so responsive and charming. And yet, in the session he presented himself as a rather unattractive man, lacking in any charisma. Was my lukewarm response to him a reflection of how unlovable *he* felt, deep inside?

To my surprise, meeting him for a second time was totally different to our first encounter. This time, James was wearing a beautifully tailored suit and, despite his slightness and thinning hair, he presented as lithe, fit and well turned out. As it was a warm September day, he immediately took off his jacket to reveal an exquisitely sculpted shirt which, I noticed, framed his slight but athletic frame perfectly. Handmade, I thought to myself. As we began talking, James seemed unrecognisable from the rather fragile and uncertain character I'd met the week before. I quickly picked up on how present he seemed to be, how much less fragile he appeared and how much more assertive he was. It was becoming clearer to me that there were two sides to James and he had decided to show me both. An unloved, unlovable James and now this confident, shiny self. What was real? What was fake?

Once he'd sat down and carefully raised his trouser leg to protect the crisp creases, he launched into telling me more of his story. He was now nearly 40, he said, and found himself, not for the first time, in a tangle between his present partner of three years, Grazyna, and two other women. He explained that he'd never really had a monogamous relationship and was given to seeing at least two if not three women at the same time. His duplicity often got found out and he was therefore regularly dumped. He rarely ended a relationship; usually the women gave up on him.

'Do you mind when you're "dumped"?' I asked.

'Not really,' James said brightly. 'It's kind of a bit upsetting but I usually know when it's coming and have started another flirtation by then.'

He explained that he thought he was addicted to the 'chase' and he felt quite bad about messing around in this way but up to now he hadn't been able to stop. He wondered if part of the problem for him was that Grazyna, felt a bit different; she was special.

'She's too good for me, Susanna. Definitely punching above my weight with her,' he said, laughing. I noticed his teeth were perfectly white and even and that they seemed to be a representation of the way he hid this darker stuff behind a glossy and charming front.

'The crunch is coming, though. She's been working in Paris but her contract is coming to an end and she's expecting to come back to London and move in with me.' He raised his eyebrows and grimaced, as though this was a ridiculous idea. 'We've been discussing and planning this for most of our relationship; it's not news.' And he laughed again, showing those perfect teeth.

'You haven't said how you feel about it, her moving in?' I said, encouraging him to look a little deeper. He smiled at me warmly and said he thought he loved her and knew it was time he settled down to have a family but he felt 'sick in his stomach' at the thought of giving up his other women.

'Is this the same feeling you have at night, James?' I asked. 'Is this the "sickness in your stomach" that is keeping you awake?' He looked at me intently, as though I'd said something extraordinary rather than making a simple and rather obvious link.

'Yes,' he exclaimed, 'now you say it, I see it. Do you think I'm not sleeping because of Grazyna? Maybe it's nothing to do with being called out like that by Steve?'

'Yes, because you seem to be saying that you're at a kind of crossroads in your life. A part of you wants to be closer and more committed to Grazyna but another part of you doesn't know if you'll be able to.' James nodded, looking thoughtful.

James's enthusiasm for my observations and the warm gratitude he expressed as the session ended left me much more hopeful about the therapy. I could sense a shift in myself and a relief that he was turning out to be so engaging and

ready to work. True, I could see things would move slowly –
he had little insight into himself and found it difficult to see
the links between his feeling states and his behaviours – but I
was now hopeful, and the work began.

Over the following weeks, I learnt that James worked in
the city leading a successful PR company; that he'd been a
'whiz kid' and made a lot of money but was now struggling
to consolidate his early success. He confessed that at university, he'd developed a problem with cocaine but had 'cleaned
up' and was now devoted to the gym and well on the way to
being completely vegan. Though work worried him from
time to time, James felt his life to be 'pretty perfect except for
the mess I'm in with women'. When I didn't respond to this
and there was a lull, James said that he'd decided before starting therapy that he'd be completely frank with me. He knew
that I couldn't help him if he didn't tell me everything.

'You need to know that no one else knows what I'm
really like. Only you. I spend a lot of time convincing others
I'm a straight-up, lovely, decent guy . . . I'm not.'

I half wondered to myself if he told me this to make me
feel special in some way and if this was one of the ways he
seduced women. But I concentrated on James's negative feelings about himself and commented that it was interesting that
he'd gone into PR, as it seemed that this was how he related
to people, as though he needed to 'curate' his public persona.
He agreed with my interpretation and said that he usually
worked hard to get people to like him. I sensed that our
working partnership was deepening as he shared more and
more.

On the other hand, James was often late for his sessions.
It wasn't unusual for me to receive a text 20 minutes before
the session was due to start telling me that he would be late,
or even that he was sorry but he wasn't going to make it at all.
More interestingly, his texts, on occasion, would ask me to

remind him what time the session was. This was most surprising as I believe strongly in what I call the three Rs of therapy: rhythm, regularity and reliability, which means that sessions are scheduled for the same time and same day every week. How could he keep forgetting, I wondered?

Psychoanalytic therapists pay close attention to the kind of relationship that is created between them and their patient; we try to notice the kinds of feelings that our patients stir up in us. Do we like them? Do we feel useless? Do we feel competitive? We notice these feelings in ourselves because sometimes they are useful clues to the patient's inner world and the way they unconsciously construct their relationships.

I noticed that James treated me in two ways. Sometimes he made me feel as if I was a very good therapist whom he could truly trust. At these times, he let me know that I was special to him and that his therapy with me was important. But at other times, he made me feel I was peripheral to what really mattered to him, that he wasn't attached to me or committed to the work we were doing together and that, at any moment, he could drop the sessions from his mind and his schedule. In other words, he blew hot and cold and I very much suspected this was how he treated many people in his life, not least the women he was involved with. Gradually, he began to tell more detail about his relationship with these two other women, Dominique and Marcie. He'd been involved with them for nearly two years and he admitted that this was very much part of a pattern, as he always had at least two relationships on the go. The affairs with Dominique and Marcie were something new, however, because they knew each other and also knew they were both sleeping with him. He left this revelation hanging and went silent and I was left sitting there wondering if he was talking about a threesome. I felt a bit teased and tantalised by what he'd told me and aware that there was a sense of excitement around this secret life. He told me just enough to pique my interest and then held back, and suddenly I realised here he was, drawing me in again, only to keep me at arm's length. It made me feel shut out and a bit useless. Noticing how he treated me gave me an insight into how he drew women to him. Perhaps this was how he'd tantalised and drawn in Grazyna, Dominique and Marcie?

'You say, James, that you've made a pact with yourself to be completely honest with me, yet I notice that you only half tell me things, that you share something and then leave it hanging. I wonder if this is your way of ensuring I stay interested and that you keep a sense of control. I think you really do want my help but you also want to keep the reins in your own hands by holding back things. If you share everything with me, then perhaps you'll feel too exposed?'

James sat with his fists in tight balls in his lap for what must have been 30 seconds. I left him with it as he was clearly chewing over my words. I could hear birds singing outside in the last throes of summer before they headed south. Eventually, James opened one of his balled fists and simply said, 'OK.'

What the 'OK' meant became clearer over the next few sessions as James tried to be more open. He described how he never actually had sex with either Dominique or Marcie but that the three of them went to group sex parties together and had sex with other people whilst watching each other. He found the parties both exciting and disturbing. He was often afraid he wouldn't be able to 'perform' but when he did, he left exhilarated and this kept him 'feeling good the whole week'. He didn't want to give up this lifestyle and indeed he doubted he would be able to, even if Grazyna came back to London and moved in with him.

One day, James turned up in an agitated state and started talking again about how his nights were still disturbed and

how, when he did manage to sleep, he was plagued by
dreams. I asked him to tell me about any he could recall. At
first, he was evasive, saying he knew the dreams were scary
and weird, but he was unable to remember any of the particu-
lars. I waited and then said, 'Really, you can't remember
anything?' He then began to describe a recurring image that
had been troubling him.

'There's this long pathway in a park with a hedgerow on
one side and oak trees on the other. I think it's Regent's Park,
where I used to run when I first came to live in London. I
know that I'm absolutely parched and I must get a drink. I
think there's a fountain nearby but I can't see it, even though
I can hear water gushing and cascading all around me. I keep
walking and walking towards the sound of the water but I
can't get any closer and can't see where it's coming from. I'm
starting to panic because I'm dying of thirst.' He stopped,
frowned and said, 'I can't remember any more. Maybe that's
when I woke up?'

I waited a bit to see if he wanted to say more and then
asked, 'What do *you* make of it?'

There was a pause.

'I lay there a long time after that dream; I couldn't get
back to sleep. I felt really uncomfortable about it and haven't
been able to get it out of my mind.' He paused again and we
were silent together. Then he said, 'The path, in the dream, is
very scary – it's a scary feeling walking to that fountain, or
whatever it is.'

I asked him if he knew why he'd been so unsure about
sharing this with me. It seemed he was quite troubled and
scared by the dream, yet I had had to press him to hear it.

He said that his nights were completely different from
his days and he wasn't sure he wanted me to know that much
about him. 'In the day, I feel generally OK, good even. But
at night, especially when I can't sleep, I feel . . .' He struggled

to find the words. 'I suppose I feel a bit pathetic telling you I've been freaked out by a stupid dream.'

I said, 'Perhaps that's what the dream is about?' He looked at me quizzically, so I went on. 'Perhaps I'm the fountain in your dream? You know you need help but find it shameful to ask for it; in the dream, you're desperate for something but feel scared to go towards it. It seems to me the dream is about your fear of needing me . . . perhaps of needing anyone?'

He looked at me intently and then simply said, 'Maybe.'

The following session, James didn't turn up. No text or call to explain. Later that evening I emailed him, saying I was sorry he hadn't come and hoped everything was OK.

It was three days before I heard back from him. He left a message to say he was sorry he'd missed the session; he'd had to go to New York for work and was still there. He hoped to see me the following week. Was this his way of stepping back from any suggestion he might really need the work with me? I thought that he was 'taking back control' and letting me know that my suggestion that he was frightened of being dependent on me had been too much. I had probably hit the mark but that didn't mean he liked it or could bear to know it.

James had told me a little about his childhood, though only when I asked. His parents had divorced when he was a baby and by the time he was aged five, both had remarried and had new families. Suddenly, he wasn't an only child but found himself surrounded by half-brothers and step-siblings. He spent his time travelling between his father's home in Wandsworth and his mother in Woking, and, from the age of eight, his boarding school in Suffolk. He said that he'd felt most at home at school but that he'd never really felt as if he belonged anywhere. In one of our sessions, he told me about a Christmas when he was aged about eleven. He'd been going to spend Christmas Day with his mother and his stepfather but at the last minute this had changed because his baby half-brother had become quite ill. His father picked him up from Woking and took him back to the Wandsworth house late on Christmas Eve. The following morning, everyone realised that all his presents had been left in Woking. He had nothing to open, no stocking or anything, and had to watch whilst everyone else opened theirs.

I felt moved listening to this memory that conveyed something deeply painful about being left out and not feeling cared for. He didn't cry as he talked to me but he reached for a tissue, breathing deeply and slowly as if attempting to gain control over his emotions.

When James returned, we began to talk more about his dislike of feeling he needed anyone. He told me he wouldn't even have a cleaner and scrubbed his own floors because he couldn't bear it when she had let him down. We explored how he feared being let down by Grazyna and I suggested maybe that was why he needed at least two girlfriends, so he could protect himself by having 'safety in numbers'. He had back-ups; if Grazyna wasn't available, he had Marcie. If Marcie was cool or distant, he had Dominique. In this way, he never had to fear being let down; he kept his distance and thereby kept them needy, so he never had to be.

During the session, we also explored why he was so attached to the sex parties. What was it about watching Marcie and Dominique that was so compelling? It seemed a complete puzzle but at the next session he began to talk about his twin half-brothers and how he'd been to watch them play a gig at the weekend. They were, he said, exceptionally talented. They'd both been in TV shows when they were children and the younger twin had also been an amazing footballer. Now they were in this folk duo and becoming quite successful. I wondered if their achievements had been hard for him when he was growing up, if he'd felt jealous and competitive with them?

'I spent a lot of time going to their games or their plays or whatever when I was growing up. It got a bit much at times,' he admitted, laughing. 'I tried to do the good big brother kind of thing but it was frustrating that no one ever seemed interested in what I was up to. I'd come home from boarding school for the weekend and then have to go and watch Danny play football or go to some stupid carol concert. And when I went to Dad's, I always seemed to end up having to go and watch Lily in some ballet performance. Not much fun for a teenage boy,' he said, smiling ruefully.

I commented that it was interesting that he felt he'd spent much of his childhood being an onlooker and reminded him of the Christmas he'd described to me, when he watched everyone open their presents, whilst he had none. I thought that this position of being on the outside, always watching, had probably been painful for him and made him feel neglected and as though he didn't really belong.

He looked at me and said, 'Yes, that's exactly the feeling I had this weekend at the concert. I watched my mother and she literally couldn't take her eyes off my brothers.'

We sat in silence for a while and then I said, 'It's striking, given what you've just described, that you seem to be taking this onlooker position at these sex parties.'

'I guess, yeah.'

We talked then about how although being an observer was difficult for him, it seemed he liked watching at the parties.

'I think at the sex parties you can be in control,' I ventured. 'You can turn the painful onlooker experience into something exciting, in which you're kind of orchestrating the whole thing. It's a way of gaining control over the thing you fear most.'

He nodded. 'Fear most?' he asked.

'Yes, the fear of being excluded; being the outsider; having no place . . .'

The fear of exclusion is a universal experience. I remember as a child how much I hated any feeling of being left out, whether it was not being chosen for the netball team or hearing my parents' absorbed conversation downstairs whilst I lay alone in bed. Even now, as a grown woman, in that awkward moment at the end of a meeting, when people break into huddles to chat, I always tremble inside, fearing I'll have no one to talk to and, as a result, I rarely wait around to find out. This anxiety about exclusion stems from our earliest realisation that our one-to-one bonds, with mothers and fathers, are not actually exclusive. They are 'playing away' with each other and with our siblings; they are 'unfaithful' to us, interested and engaged with others. What a tragedy. What a betrayal. We don't come first! This is a shocking, painful and potentially life-threatening realisation, because when this discovery is made, we are, in fact, completely dependent on our parents. Dependent for food, for shelter, for care and, indeed, for survival itself. For many people, intimate relationships revive these early terrors and a confusion between adult dependency and infantile dependency ensues. This confusion, which stimulates deep fears around survival, drives us to protect ourselves from this terror by building walls and defences that help us avoid any situation where we might feel dependent and vulnerable.

In James's case, this meant developing a persona that hid his fragility and through which he could charm and manipulate his lovers, thereby maintaining an illusion of control. But the saddest part is that the thing he feared most, the catastrophe he was trying to avoid, of being desperate and helpless like an infant, had, in fact, already happened. Donald Winnicott, the wise psychoanalyst who has written so eloquently about a child's inner world, explains that when traumatic things happen to us in infancy it is impossible for us to make sense of and process the experience. At that stage in life, infants simply aren't equipped to reflect and understand all the feelings linked to the trauma. And so, adults who've experienced trauma in infancy carry these unprocessed feelings into adulthood; they sit deep inside them as a fear about a disaster that is coming, when in fact it's already happened.

For James, it seemed this trauma had occurred around the breakdown of his parents' marriage and the consequent loss of a secure base that made him feel safe and held. Over the months, as we explored his childhood, I got such an acute sense of a very little boy shuffled between his mother and father, both of whom were preoccupied with themselves, their new partners and their new babies. It was as though, too early, he'd been dropped from his parents' minds and, unable to cope with these feelings of exclusion and rejection, he had built a castle inside himself to protect him from the pain.

Did this understanding mark a turning point? Things seemed to carry on pretty much as before, except that he began to talk about Grazyna. For the first time, I had a sense of her as a real person and I started to see just how involved James was with her.

It was March when the crisis happened. It was something I'd been half expecting and in hindsight was almost inevitable. It was a Sunday evening when James texted me to ask if he could see me urgently; he couldn't wait until Thursday. Grazyna had found out about him and Marcie and she'd broken it off. I texted him back and we agreed to meet on Tuesday.

James looked broken when he arrived – not crisp and assured but fragile and uncared for. Straight away, he launched into telling me he'd been in Paris with Grazyna. He'd arrived late and gone straight into the shower, leaving his mobile phone on the kitchen counter right by where Grazyna was preparing him dinner. His phone had pinged and Grazyna had picked it up and seen a suggestive message from Marcie, which clearly signalled there was something sexual between them.

This time, in the consulting room, James did cry. What was he to do? He'd fucked everything up and it was all hopeless. He'd been trying to get straight by coming to see me but now it was too late and he'd lost Grazyna.

Two days later, he was back for his regular session. He was in a tracksuit and said he'd taken a couple of days off work to go and see Grazyna in Paris. She was still very angry with him but he was hopeful he might win her back. He told me he'd had the dream again. Again, he was in the park and there was a fountain and he wanted to drink but couldn't find the water. This time, however, he saw the fountain – it was one of those huge Victorian tiered ones. It was bright and white and looked like it was fragile and could crumble. He still couldn't reach it though and he was still desperate to drink.

I asked him if he had any more thoughts about the dream and about the fountain and he said that actually it looked like an enormous cake. 'A wedding cake?' I asked. And he nodded vigorously – yes, just like that.

In July, nearly a year after we began work, Grazyna moved in with him and when I returned in September, he came eagerly to the session to tell me she was pregnant. Something had shifted in him but both of us knew that the work we were doing together was by no means finished.

James's journey towards marriage involved a confrontation with the need and vulnerability he'd worked hard his whole life to avoid. Through the affairs and the casual use of women, he'd maintained an illusion of power and control, triumphing over the part of him that he hated and felt was too needy and fragile. In the therapy, these different parts of him were exposed and through this sense of being held and known, he began the process of understanding and accepting his ordinary human need for love and security.

RED RIDING HOOD
PROTECTS THE WOLF IN
SHEEP'S CLOTHING

Betrayal is a fact of life; I doubt there is an adult alive that hasn't felt its sting. To trust someone always poses a risk of treachery; realistic trust involves knowing and accepting this. But accepting that loved ones will, at times, lie, cheat or let you down, doesn't mean that every betrayal is forgivable.

Pippa and Claudine, a married couple in their early forties, came to see me because for several years Claudine had been suffering with a mysterious ME-like illness, which, from time to time, made her extremely ill. For nearly three years, Claudine had been investigated for strokes, asthma, multiple sclerosis and labyrinthitis – all conditions that might have explained why, at times, she would lose her balance and fall, black out or take to her bed with exhaustion. The tests found nothing conclusive, so the couple developed an understanding between them that Claudine had an atypical form of chronic fatigue syndrome or, as it's sometimes called, ME.

Some months after this 'diagnosis', Claudine seemed to become increasingly unwell, which resulted in her becoming bed bound. She was unable to work or help in the house, prompting Pippa, in despair, to insist on further tests. Referred by their GP, Claudine underwent more hospital investigations, which once again drew a blank. No medical professional was able to identify any underlying condition that could account for her complete exhaustion, her occasional fainting fits and the myriad other symptoms she was suffering from.

Months passed and Claudine remained an invalid until a good friend suggested to Pippa that they try another specialist who worked in Paris. This doctor ran a clinic specifically dedicated to chronic, disabling and diffuse conditions, such as seemed to be afflicting Claudine. It was expensive and money was tight but there appeared to be no other option but to give it a try.

In the meantime, Pippa had been supporting the family financially and managing the household, caring not only for Claudine but also for Claudine's 12-year-old daughter, Milly. Pippa was becoming frantic with worry, fearful that Claudine would never get well and without a diagnosis, she fretted that something terrible was about to happen, even that Claudine might die.

Eventually the money was found and, leaving Milly behind with a friend, the couple travelled to Paris. Despite the nature of the trip, they were excited. They'd never been on the Eurostar before and it was years since they'd been away from home alone. At the first appointment, the nurse took some blood and urine. The results, later that day, were as shocking as they were devastating. Claudine had an extremely high reading for opioids. Was this an aberration? What could it mean?

They spent a hellish night, with tearful accusations and tearful denials, but the following morning, in the presence of the doctor, Claudine finally confessed she'd been abusing opioid painkillers for years. Her consumption had varied but she had avoided taking the medications entirely only when she'd been having tests. She didn't have atypical MS, or some other unknown ailment, she was, simply, a drug addict. At this moment of crisis, as Claudine emerged from her detox, they sought therapy with me.

This dishonesty felt to Pippa like a monstrous betrayal and she told me that Claudine's secret drug abuse felt as unforgivable as any affair. Pippa confessed in that first session that she was on the verge of initiating a separation and I couldn't help thinking that I really didn't blame her. But any idea of leaving was impossible because Claudine, in the face of this threat, would withdraw into the most profound and deathly silence that scared Pippa witless.

It was quite a challenge to hold onto the position central to any couple therapist of interest and attention to the *shared* aspects of the presenting issues as, in those early sessions, I felt downright punitive towards Claudine and protective of Pippa. But gradually, it began to be clear that there had been a strong, unconscious collusion between the couple and I could see that Pippa had turned a very blind eye to Claudine's drug abuse in order to avoid something much worse.

As they talked more about the past and as Pippa railed against the lies, I began to wonder why Pippa had ignored so many tell-tale signs. Why had she overlooked the withdrawal of cash from their bank account with no satisfactory explanation? I felt sceptical when Pippa told me that she'd believed that the pill bottles she found hidden behind the shed had been chucked over the fence by local kids, as Claudine asserted. It became more and more clear that Pippa had overlooked all the signs. What was less clear was why.

It took some weeks for us to talk about anything other than the drug taking and the lies. Every session was hot with anger and shame, which left no room for gentle exploration. But during one session, as I became more and more puzzled by this couple, I insisted that they make space, between the forensic examination of the betrayals, to tell me something about their childhood and their families.

'I'm not sure Claudine will be up for talking about it, will you?' Pippa said protectively. 'I can tell you about mine though, if that's of any help?' Pippa was always like this, chatty and co-operative, whilst Claudine was often very silent. I nodded and Pippa began.

'Gosh. I haven't really thought about *my* family for years! I see my sister from time to time but never my brother or my dad. My brother lives in Oman. My dad, well, he's a real odd-ball. I don't think he wants to see me and I don't want to see him either. It's mutual!' she concluded, laughing. I waited, hoping she'd say more, but she seemed to think that was enough and nudged Claudine with her elbow to get her to talk. 'Claudine's got a real story. She had a tough time grow-ing up.'

Claudine was no more forthcoming than Pippa but reluctantly she told me she'd been in and out of care during her childhood, until, at 12, she was fostered and then adopted by Delia, who she now thought of as her mum. She'd not seen or heard from either of her blood parents for years but when Milly was born, she'd got in contact with her biological mother.

'It was a mistake. I thought maybe she'd be older, wiser, more up for being a grandma or something. But she's just not someone I want anything to do with now.'

'Why were you taken into care, Claudine? Do you know?' I asked, wondering what she'd suffered as a child.

'I've been told that I was about one, the first time I went into care. My mum was using heroin and she was still with my dad.' She paused, pressing her lips firmly together and, like Pippa, it was clear she wanted to leave it there, so I didn't push her.

After they left, I made my way upstairs. The day was turning out colder than I'd thought and I needed to retrieve a cardigan before I saw my next patient. I put on the cardigan and went to the mirror and, as I stood by it, near the open window, I could hear a loud voice in the street below. Look-ing out, I saw Pippa and Claudine standing by a beaten-up old green Fiat across the road. Pippa's voice was raised and though I couldn't hear her words, I could hear the tone and I could see from Claudine's shrunken and slumped profile that she was in receipt of a serious telling-off.

As we went on with the therapy, the little bit of their childhood history they'd shared began to help me make sense of their intense and lopsided relationship. It was evident that Claudine behaved in many ways like a child. Even now, though she claimed to have stopped abusing drugs for nearly six months, Pippa would bring her breakfast in bed. Claudine, who was a freelance editor, had begun to take on projects again but she struggled to complete and finish the work. Then Pippa would step in to help her and Claudine would immediately step back and allow her to do so. Claudine clearly wanted – needed, perhaps – for Pippa to mummy her and being helpless triggered that attention. Her drug abuse had tamped down painful feelings and collapsed her into a dependent, childlike state, secure in the knowledge that Pippa would be there to catch her.

One Tuesday morning, the air cold but the sky bright, Pippa arrived on her own. Claudine, it seemed, wouldn't get out of bed to come to the session. I felt irritated with Claudine and that irritation increased as I heard how Pippa had tried to rouse her, had taken her breakfast, had dropped Milly at school, had gone back and brought her a cup of coffee – but all to no avail. Claudine wasn't getting out of bed.

'Do you think she's been using?' I asked.

'I don't think so. No. She wouldn't do that. I'm sure she wouldn't,' Pippa said, shaking her head. There was a silence between us and I watched as Pippa took in my question properly.

'Why would you say that?' Her voice was querulous.

'Well, I might ask why you haven't considered that?'

'I don't think you understand what's been going on.

There's no way Claud would use now. She knows it would break my heart.'

I sat silently. I knew that she had to find her own way to her doubt.

'I don't know. I don't know what to say. What d'you want me to say?' she said angrily.

'I don't want you to say anything, Pippa, but I do notice that it seems difficult for you to acknowledge or even allow yourself to feel *any* frustration or anger with Claudine. It seems easier to direct it at me. And I do wonder why that might be?'

'She's trying and you don't seem to get how hard it is for her.'

'I understand it's incredibly hard for her. My question is why you ignore how hard it is, and how hard it's been, for *you*?'

She bowed her head and we sat there in silence. I looked at her and thought how tired and sad she looked. Her greying black hair was scraped back into a ponytail and her hands, which were folded in her lap, looked red and sore, the finger-nails bitten to the quick.

'You've never really told me much about your childhood or your family Pippa.'

'Mine? I did tell you.'

'Not really. Just that you don't really see them.'

She sighed and shrugged her shoulders. 'Well, it wasn't great, if that's what you're thinking. My dad was, *is*, a complete loser. Did I tell you my mum died when I was 12? I've been thinking she might have been an alcoholic, though, frankly, being married to him I don't blame her . . .'

It took time but, over the session, she was able to give me a graphic picture of a childhood in which, as the oldest of four, she'd habitually stepped in as 'little mother'. Her father, though a steady earner, had never behaved like an adult; he was funny and playful but would come and go erratically and seemed incapable of taking any responsibility.

'And your mother?' I asked.

'I loved my mum,' Pippa said simply. 'She could be really fun. Sometimes she was frightening, though.'

'Frightening?'

'Yeah. She'd . . . well, lose it and then, oh, you wanted to get out of her way.'

'I wonder if you spent a lot of time trying to make sure she didn't lose it?' Pippa looked at me, puzzled. 'By taking over, by mummying *her*. By soothing *her*?' I suggested.

Pippa nodded. 'Yeah. That's right. Spot on. I'd do anything to keep her calm. I remember once she got really raging about the ants in the kitchen. She was jumping up and down and chucking boiling water all the over the place.' Pippa laughed.

'It sounds more scary than funny,' I said, smiling ruefully.

'Yeah, true. My brother got burnt. I told the ambulance man it was me . . . with the boiling water.' She shrugged.

As the session went on, she told me that her mother had died quite suddenly from blood poisoning. She'd gone to the doctor with a bad pain in her arm but was told it was a pulled muscle strain. Three days later, she died in hospital of sepsis. After that, 12-year-old Pippa became the 'little mother' of the family. Her father absented himself, leaving her in charge of her siblings. She became a little soldier mummy protecting her 'brood'.

'When you told the ambulance man it was you who'd burnt your brother, I think you were trying to protect your mother. And perhaps trying to keep her as a "good" mummy in your mind. I think you do the same thing with Claudine. You try to protect her and you try to keep her as a "good" wife in your mind.'

'She is good, Susanna. She's just . . .' She searched for a word. 'Damaged.'

Was Pippa repeating her childhood with Claudine, falling into a pattern of behaviour that felt familiar and known? I've never found the idea of repetition compulsion, in which a person keeps repeating something because it's familiar, a satisfactory theory. Surely natural selection would have evolved that habit out of us? But at the heart of all my work is a recognition that people *do* seem to choose partners whose experience in childhood almost always in some way echoes their own. Why would this be so? Why would Pippa choose Claudine – someone, though lovable in many ways, who required just the kind of devotion and attention that Pippa's mother demanded? Surely Pippa should have run a mile? Surely Pippa should have found someone who'd look after *her*?

Soon after this session, I managed to find a good colleague to work with Claudine. We'd been talking about how important it was that Claudine had some therapy on her own and now it seemed she was ready. She began to see her own therapist twice a week and it didn't take long for that to shift things.

'I'm finding these sessions aren't really helping me anymore. I think we should stop coming,' Claudine suddenly announced one autumn day as our session began.

Pippa, still shrugging off her blue denim jacket, looked shocked. 'You didn't say that to me. You can't just decide that on your own! *I* don't want to stop coming, Claud.'

'Well, *you* continue with Susanna. *I* don't have to. I've got my own therapist now.'

'Perhaps three sessions a week feels a little intense, Claudine?' I asked gently, pushing down a flash of anger at her precipitous and high-handed decision.

Before Claudine could reply, Pippa, picking up my

thread, jumped back in. 'If it's too much, sweetie, we can stop. I'm sorry. I don't want you to feel under pressure from me. You've got a lot on your plate dealing with everything.'

'Why don't you want to go on your own?' Claudine asked.

Pippa cocked her head and looked at me and then back at Claudine, as though considering the idea. 'I don't think so. What for? Perhaps we *should* just stop. Or stop for a bit?' And she looked at me again, checking my reaction.

'Are you both saying that there isn't a problem in the relationship anymore? Or that the problems have really been just Claudine's problems?'

Pippa nodded but without any great enthusiasm.

'We've discussed before, the way that Pippa has been a mother substitute to you, Claudine, but now you've started with your own therapist, perhaps it feels as though you're getting enough of being mummied? And coming to see me is just one mummy too many?'

Claudine laughed and nodded her head. 'Maybe, maybe. I just don't always want to be the one who's the centre of attention, you know.'

After that, we explored what it meant to be the centre of attention both at home and in the therapy with me. Claudine acknowledged she liked Pippa taking care of her but she didn't like the way Pippa didn't take her seriously. She complained that Pippa bossed her around and then they skirmished around who made decisions about Milly. I listened carefully and remembered the scene that I'd witnessed outside my window; it seemed that Claudine had begun to recognise that there was a cost as well as a benefit to being a child in this relationship.

Eventually, I said that although it might seem as if sorting out Claudine would sort out their problems, I thought there was something important in the dynamic between them they needed to address.

'My therapist thinks Pippa's got a lot of problems. Not just me. It feels like it's always just me who's got to do the changing. What about you, Pippa?' Claudine said, glaring at me.

'You think I've been part of making *you* the problem? Letting Pippa off the hook?' I asked.

'Well, you have. Sort of, yeah. I know you're saying now about it being both of us but you haven't been, not usually,' Claudine said bluntly.

I had to admit to myself there was probably some truth in this. I didn't really like her – or rather, I didn't approve of her. I knew this wasn't right, that I wasn't being even-handed or fair, but it was a struggle. She seemed so arrogant and selfish and Pippa, though avoidant in some ways, was so much easier to like.

We didn't come to any conclusions that session and they left me with the understanding that they'd be back the following week to discuss it further. I felt irritated. That flash of anger at Claudine now felt directed at them both. It felt like they were washing their hands of the therapy and me, and that things would continue as before without any desire for any real change. I was struck how quickly Pippa had reverted to denying her own needs and jumped to protecting Claudine, even when she behaved like a spoilt and selfish child.

Two days later, I got an email from Pippa:

Dear Susanna,

I hope you're well. I'm just dropping you a line to say that we've decided to pause the therapy. I think you were spot on when you said it was feeling too much for Claud and so, for now, I think we should stop. Thank you so much for all the help you've given us at such a difficult time. We really appreciate it.

Pippa

Why is it that some couples will stick with therapy through hell and high water whilst others turn away? I could see that I'd probably focused too much on Claudine and her problems and unconsciously nominated her as the 'ill' patient with Pippa as her victim. It was understandable that she was fed up with feeling she was always in the doghouse but why did Pippa decide to back away too? Was it the thought of change? Was the therapy beginning to unravel the collusion between them and was it this that was being resisted? Whilst the burden of caring for Claudine was considerable, Pippa, in her grown-up role, got to feel in control and strong. Though her needs were put on hold, she could distance herself from her own childlike fragility by being a loving, if sometimes controlling and bossy, mummy.

As I contemplated this, I thought about the walk I'd taken the previous weekend with my nervous, rather urban friend in the countryside outside of London. We were chatting away when we reached a field full of cows. My friend demurred – she hated cows, was terrified of them, and proceeded to tell me that today's cows were, because of breeding, far more dangerous than cows of the past. These weren't docile, doe-eyed Daisies with a charming bell around their throats; these, she said, were anxious and unpredictable beasts and we must find another way through. But there was no other way through, no detour or alternative route. We either went through the field or we turned back and gave up on the rather nice pub lunch awaiting us at the end of the walk. Whilst I am no hero, not brave or athletic, her anxious pleading made me feel strong and determined. Gathering myself, I reassured her in an authoritative voice and we made our way through the field at a brisk pace and out the other side. I felt triumphant and fearless; all my own anxiety had evaporated, so firmly had I projected it into her.

Pippa's own fragility was lodged in Claudine and by caring for her lover as if she was a small, helpless baby, she vicariously cared for herself too. But though we'd begun to understand the underlying causes of Claudine's addictions and I had begun to explore Pippa's part in the deception, I still wondered if Claudine's lies were forgivable. And if they were, what would make true forgiveness possible? Claudine had allowed Pippa to fuss over her, to make doctor's appointments, ignoring the pain and anxiety she was creating. Claudine had watched Pippa work herself to the bone to keep a roof over their heads, struggling to care for them all, whilst, all the time, she was secretly abusing drugs. And, in all the time she attended therapy, she never really said sorry.

Psychotherapists are trained not to take moral stands; we need to remain curious and open even in the presence of grand immorality. That isn't to say that psychoanalytic therapy is amoral; indeed, psychoanalysis aims to help patients confront their destructiveness head on and, in time, take responsibility for the damage done. I'd failed to help Claudine face the hurt she'd caused and failed to help Pippa stand her ground in expecting some repentance. I had the sense that Pippa would do her best to keep Claudine, whatever the consequences, but, as a result, they wouldn't be any closer or trusting.

How *do* couples recover well from great betrayals? Is it possible and is it wise? First and foremost, there needs to be the recognition that there *has* been a betrayal and that there is an accompanying sense of remorse about it. Say sorry. Then say sorry again and mean it. I have seen couples where the betrayal has been revealed and lies exposed but the betrayer continues to deny it. They cannot face and own their guilt, so they leave their partner not only with the trauma of having been let down but the further pain of that trauma not being recognised. In this situation, the hurt cannot heal and the couple cannot regain any sense of trust. Restoring trust takes time; a partner needs months and years of good experiences with their lover to gradually rub down the sharp edge of doubt and uncertainty. They need to believe that the betrayal won't be repeated, that it is in the past or was a one-time thing. The restoration of a good sex life also helps because, of course, a less than satisfactory sex life is a very common reason for an affair in the first place. Finally, I've noticed that the couples who do best after a betrayal are those who, together, develop a narrative around the 'why'. These couples take shared ownership of the root causes of the betrayal, acknowledging that the relationship was in a shaky state even before the duplicity and come to an understanding that the affair was a symptom of those problems.

PART THREE
FLESH AND BLOOD

Come away, O human child!
To the waters and the wild
With a faery, hand in hand,
For the world's more full of weeping than you can
  understand.

> —W. B. Yeats, 'The Stolen Child',
> *The Wanderings of Oisin and Other Poems*

Flesh and blood is gory – just like family life. Family life begins after the fairy tale ends. Though many couples will live happily, they will not live happily *always*. There is no 'ever after' about it.

The arrival or non-arrival of children is most usually the problem. They are wanted, needed, but they are so dependent and for so, so long. Having children is the most challenging part of being a couple because being a good-enough parent means sacrifice; it means budging up and letting someone else in. It means meeting parts of yourself long buried in infancy and childhood – how else would we know what our children feel? What our children need?

And families? It seems we need them to flourish. They ground us, give us a place to belong and form our identities. Family links our past with our present and family holds the key to our future. Family is the place where we can try and rework that past and repair our pain, and all the pain and struggle of our ancestors, in an endless sequence of generations.

BINA AND SHAPIRO CONJURE UP A BABY

The email from Bina asking for couple therapy was particularly polite. In every correspondence, she managed to convey that she was a thoughtful, respectful person. She was very understanding when I said I was currently full and seemed perfectly happy to wait for an appointment. She signed off her emails with *Warmest Wishes, Bina* ♡. The heart seemed overkill but, nonetheless, I was looking forward to meeting Bina and her husband Shapiro.

They arrived promptly, an attractive couple, well dressed and well spoken, who smiled warmly when I gestured for them to come into my office. When I asked them to tell me a little about why they'd come, they smiled again and turned to each other to agree who'd start.

'Good question,' Shapiro said approvingly, pointing his finger at me. 'Let me put it in a nutshell. I think there are three points we need to address.' He looked at Bina, who nodded agreement. 'One,' he raised his thumb. 'How and when are we going to start a family? Two,' he raised his forefinger, 'What do we mean by quality time and how do we get to a mutual agreement around that? And three, how do we negotiate the financial and homemaking balance between us once we've started our family? In other words, Susanna, we need *you* to help *us* get to a "Version 2.0" of this relationship and we need some quick wins. We don't want to boil the ocean over this, we've done some work already on getting the questions right. We just need you to set us off in the right direction. Right, hon?' Shapiro stopped and checked in with Bina, who, again, smiled and nodded. Then Shapiro, neatly dressed in his grey suit and matching greying hair, sat back and waited for me to come up with a plan.

It's unusual for me to be lost for words but I have to admit Shapiro had succeeded in striking me dumb. My heart sank and I had little idea what he was talking about. All I could feel was the powerful wish in them for a quick solution, something I knew I wasn't able to give.

'You seem to be saying that you're both on the same page about what you want from coming to see me and I think I hear that some of this is about a life transition you're wanting to make? You want to start a family?'

They both nodded.

'Could you tell me a little more about what's been going on between you recently? Have you been at odds? Are there things you don't agree on? Might this be the reason you decided to come and see me?'

Again, they looked at each other to see who might take my question and I had the sudden peculiar feeling that I was in a conference room and they, the speakers, were taking questions from me, the audience.

'I think we've sought you out because of your reputation. We went into this very carefully and your name kept coming up. We tried one other therapist but she was full, so you were second on our list.' Shapiro beamed at me, as though congratulating me on my success. 'We don't want to mess around here. We want to get things sorted and some agreements on the table . . . if that's OK with you?'

I felt floored. This felt like a difficult mix of flattery and control that I wasn't sure how to address. I said nothing and I could see that Bina was beginning to find that uncomfortable, as she looked nervously from me to Shapiro, as though expecting trouble.

'Is it hard to "negotiate" things in your relationship, Bina?' I addressed her directly.

And then Bina began to speak, haltingly at first, but gradually she explained that Shapiro wanted them to have a baby but she wasn't sure that this was the right time for her. She'd just moved jobs and been promoted and was now poised to make a big acquisition; she needed this deal to go through before she took time off. She didn't think she'd be able to get pregnant before next March.

'I've told you, hon, next March won't work. We'll be opening the New York office then and I won't be available. If we get going now, it works much better for me and hopefully you'll be able to get the deal sewn up by Christmas. Which would mean the baby would arrive in May and I'll have the New York office up and running and you'll be able to take time off during the summer.'

I listened in astonishment. Both Bina and Shapiro seemed under the illusion that a baby could be timed exactly, like boiling an egg.

'It seems that thinking about having a baby is filled with complications and challenges for you both. And I'm wondering if this scheduling you're doing is a way to manage the uncertainty of trying for a baby?'

They both looked at me perplexed. 'We haven't actually started trying yet,' Bina responded. 'But I got pregnant last year by accident so we know we can.'

'Yep. No problems to report there!' Shapiro said brightly.

'You terminated the pregnancy?' I asked gently.

'Yes. Tricky. But the right decision at the right time,' Shapiro said, and didn't elaborate further.

Neither of them seemed to have consciously considered that getting pregnant might not be straightforward, so over the rest of the session, I tried to understand their worries about becoming parents, giving them some space to explore their feelings about this and the abortion they'd had the previous year. It was like pushing sand uphill and I sensed that Shapiro found my questions not only demanding but annoying. He wanted me to get on board with 'negotiating an agreement' between them and didn't at all see the point of exploring their pasts or their feelings about it. By the end of the session, all my attempts to get the couple to think and feel had been rebuffed. I didn't expect to see them again. I felt I'd gone from second best therapist to the bottom of the pile – from magic to tragic in their estimation.

But the next morning I received the following email:

> *Hi Susanna,*
>
> *We just loved the session yesterday and we would like to meet you for five sessions. Our only problem is that next week I'm in the US and the following week Shapiro is in Paris. So, we'd like to start in three weeks and can we meet at 5.30pm instead of 5pm? Finally, if we book for five sessions do you give a discount?*
>
> > *Great working with you.*
>
> *Bina* ♡

I wrote back firmly but politely explaining that I couldn't see them at 5.30pm, that I didn't work to a specific number of sessions or give discounts but that I could hold the session for them for two weeks. I was beginning to get a picture of this couple that made me curious. They clearly really liked to feel that they had everything nailed down and controlled. Would they be able to settle into therapy with me? I doubted it. But could I help them to become a little less action-orientated and more thoughtful, maybe?

Three weeks later, they were back. Once again, there were broad smiles as they entered and Shapiro offered his hand to shake in greeting. I took it briefly and waited for them to settle themselves on the couch. Bina looked very groomed; her lustrous jet-black hair shone as though she'd just walked out of the hairdresser's and her deep brown skin looked as though it had been polished. She was as slim as a pin and her hands were expertly manicured and varnished, two diamond bands decorating her ring finger.

They looked at me expectantly as though I was about to bring out a bag of magic tricks to conjure with but as we went on, our conversation seemed to falter – every avenue I tried to explore was shut down and every thought I offered was wrong. The sweet politeness they'd shown in the first session seemed to have evaporated. Eventually, I said, 'Maybe it feels uncomfortable for you to be needing my help . . . any help, actually. My guess is that you're used to managing things yourselves, getting on with it, sorting things and moving on. But perhaps this – your relationship – is something different? Something that needs a different kind of approach. One that involves talking about things you usually avoid and feeling things you don't usually allow yourselves to feel?'

Almost before I finished speaking, Shapiro interrupted. 'I think you're right, Susanna. Maybe we do need to do a deep dive here.'

I tried to ignore his business jargon – maybe he was acknowledging in his own way that they were blocking any exploration. Then I noticed that tears were silently running down Bina's face.

Shapiro leaned over and reached for the tissue box, which he waved in her direction for her to take. She was oblivious to him, lost in her own thoughts, so he rested the tissues precariously on the couch next to her. He looked awkward and upset. We waited.

'Sorry, sorry,' Bina said, taking a tissue and blowing her nose. 'I don't know why I'm crying. I just think it's because sometimes . . .' she paused and looked intently at Shapiro, '. . . sometimes it just seems hopeless.'

'Hopeless?' I asked.

'I just don't see how I'm going to make Shapiro happy. He seems so sure about everything and I don't think I am. I want a baby . . . I think. But I'm not sure I'm cut out for doing mother stuff *and* working. My own mother didn't work and she was *always* exhausted. *And* there was a lot of help in the house. I just can't see how I'm going to manage it all.'

'We'll have help, Bee, of course we'll have help. We can have two nannies if you want. Help isn't a problem. I know your career is the most important thing. Don't sweat about that,' Shapiro tried to reassure her.

Bina then started to talk at length about her career and what it meant to her. She was clearly both successful and driven, despite having left school at 17. As she described it, I had the sense that her entire life centred on her work. She talked about the years and years of slog to prove herself but now she knew she was extremely good at her job.

I began to ponder if Bina and Shapiro were finding themselves at different stages in their development and whether this could spell danger for their relationship. It seemed that the two of them had had a shared culture, where hard work and the achievements that hard work brought had been paramount. They'd clearly invested a huge amount into their careers and Bina was now wondering whether that investment was being threatened. Shapiro, on the other hand, seemed to treat the baby 'project' almost like a kind of work challenge, driving ahead despite Bina's uncertainties. I thought they were having a conversation that was clearly at cross purposes and their shared vision of their future was beginning to unravel.

Differences in development are common reasons for couples to seek help and it can be extremely befuddling when your partner changes their feelings, wishes and ideas. If the interests, opinions and needs of one partner suddenly change, it can challenge the status quo. There are myriad things that can create this lopsided development but planning for and having children is frequently the biggest test a couple ever face. Pregnancy, birth, breastfeeding and the realities of parenthood set off physical, psychological and life changes that can put couples at odds with each other as they express their differing needs and expectations.

As they left, Shapiro looked stricken and grumpy. I'd made a last comment that questioned whether they might want quite different things and I had the distinct feeling he hadn't appreciated that at all. I liked Shapiro but, although he thought he was giving Bina everything she might desire, though he believed he was reassuring her that everything would be OK, I felt he wasn't really listening.

Shapiro and Bina continued to turn up promptly for their sessions but, despite their diligent attendance, we still seemed to be getting nowhere. At times, I had a good feeling that I'd made a connection with Bina but then if I attempted to get any closer to her, she seemed to find a way to brush me off. It was becoming clearer to me that any kind of intimacy was a challenge and whenever I felt she was becoming more emotionally available, she'd suddenly turn thoroughly sarcastic or brusque.

In the first or second session, I always ask my patients to tell me a little about their childhoods. Often, however, it takes many months, even years, to get a real picture, as patients gradually begin to remember more, trust more and slowly face the links between the past and their current struggles. It was no different with Bina and Shapiro. I asked them to tell me about their early family life and they certainly complied but, strangely, I found myself unable to recall any of the details they'd told me. When I looked back at my notes, they were also vague. Oddly, I'd scribbled down in pencil rather than typing them up and my writing was indistinct and messy. I knew that they'd told me they'd happy childhoods with parents whose marriages had thrived. I knew they both had siblings, though I was unsure how many. I knew they'd both gone to boarding school but I hadn't written at what age. In summary, despite meeting for six sessions, it felt that I didn't really know them at all. Was this my fault? Had I not been paying attention? Or perhaps it reflected the lack of connection they made with themselves, each other and me? Their lives were busy but felt completely colourless. The faded pencil scribbles seemed to sum up how indistinct and empty it seemed.

I did have some important knowledge that came from how they treated me and the work I was trying to help them do. I could feel they hated the kind of therapy I was offering. They were uncomfortable with my belief that we needed to keep things open and exploratory rather than having a specific goal or aim. It wasn't like the meetings they were used to – there was no agenda and no action points – and I could see they found this both frustrating and confusing. What kind of childhood experience, I wondered, had led to this fearful rigidity? It felt as though they'd been schooled to mistrust the world of emotions and discouraged from taking their feelings seriously. As a result, they maintained an emotional distance from me, from each other and, it seemed, even from themselves. As the sessions went on, I knew, though they didn't tell me directly, that they were increasingly distrustful of my approach. They wanted to be free of me and their need of me.

Session six arrived and I wondered what would happen next? It seemed to me increasingly likely that they'd stick to their original plan to have just six sessions, even though I felt they needed so much more. Because they were usually very prompt, I was concerned when the big hand slid past the hour on my clock and by the time it reached ten past, I felt sure that they weren't coming back. I sat there, quite disappointed; it'd been hard work to engage them and they'd resisted all my attempts to get them to open up but I felt warm towards them and still thought that there was useful work we could do together. However, I had a strong sense of how uncomfortable the sessions had been for them, so it was unsurprising that they'd dropped out. It *was* strange that they hadn't written to tell me, though; they always seemed so polite and businesslike. Was there a confusion? Did they think that they'd had the full course of sessions and that the therapy then just stopped? I thought we were on session six but perhaps they thought last week was session six? I was pondering all this as I began to compose an email, when the buzzer sounded, startling me out of my reverie.

Seconds later, Shapiro came through my door. 'Just me, hope that's OK?' he said as he took off his coat. 'I don't think Bee's coming. I waited for her at the end of the road, she's never late. I've tried ringing her . . . and texting,' he explained, looking anxiously at his phone.

'You were expecting her, then?' I asked.

'Mmm. Not sure. She has a big presentation tomorrow; she's probably stuck at work. And, to be brutally honest, she wasn't keen to come. She said there was no point coming to the last session. Nothing's gonna change.' He shrugged and looked again at his phone and then it beeped as a message came in. 'She says she's not coming,' he said, lifting his head. 'Perhaps I should go too? Not much point in me being here without her, is there?' I heard this as an appeal to me, I felt he was indicating he didn't really want to go and did want to talk.

'Perhaps there are things you'd like to talk about on your own?' I asked.

In response, Shapiro leant back on the couch, making himself more comfortable. 'I did want to ask you something,' he said.

I waited patiently, watching the uncertainty flicker across his face. After a little while and following some general comments, he began to talk about his previous relationships. He reminded me that he was nine years older than Bina and that whilst she'd never been in a serious relationship before, he'd previously been married. He was worried that history was repeating itself but in reverse. When I looked puzzled, he explained that his first marriage had ended because she'd wanted children and he didn't. They'd fought about it for months and then, despite his reluctance, she got pregnant. At first, he'd been angry and upset, but he was just getting used to the idea when, at 13 weeks, she miscarried. After that, everything seemed wrong between them and they decided to go their separate ways. She was married now to an old school friend of his and had lots of children. He joked about her trying for a rugby team and tried to laugh but he looked rueful and regretful as he recounted this tale. We sat in silence for a little while and I felt sad and sorry that I hadn't helped him talk about this before. This was the first glimpse of something more real and vulnerable. Was it safer to tell me this without Bina's presence? Was it easier to be more open given this was the last session?

'It's striking we haven't talked about this before, it's obviously very important. Does Bina know about this?' I asked.

'Yeah, yeah, absolutely. I mean, we discussed how neither of us was keen on children right at the beginning of the relationship. But then, well, we both changed our minds . . . or, at least, I thought we'd both changed our minds.' He trailed off, looking depressed. 'Do you think I should give up? On having kids, I mean. I don't want us to break up over it. I think I may've pushed Bee a bit too hard. Time to put on the brakes. Row back?' he asked.

'And what would you do about the bit of you that really wants to have a child, Shapiro?' I asked.

He looked uncertain.

'What I do notice, Shapiro, and I've said this to you before, is that it seems you really don't like uncertainty. You always push to make a decision, to act, to decide . . . when perhaps it's still a time for thinking?'

He nodded in agreement and then began to talk about his work and how his love of a solution had, at times, got him into trouble. He was beginning to realise that, as a boss, it was sometimes best to do nothing.

'I've got this guy who's working for me, running this big IT project we're doing. He comes into my office at least once a day and just rabbits on about what's broken or what doesn't work or who's not doing their job or . . . well, it's one problem after another and it's been really getting to me. I've been working my arse off to solve these issues and then, next day, BOOM! It's all sorted but not in the way I suggested, it's just got sorted. And I've realised this last couple of weeks – he doesn't need me to do anything, to sort it out for him, he just needs me to . . . listen.'

'Perhaps, you're also talking about what you need from me, from this therapy? Not a solution, but a place to sort out your thoughts and feelings . . . for me to listen?'

My comment seemed to free him up because for the rest of the session he talked without pause, as though a dam had broken and he could, at last, explore all the worries and concerns about his relationship with Bina. As we came to a close,

I suggested that perhaps they needed more time to explore all these things together and that we should go on.

'I'd very much like to, Susanna, but I'm not sure I'll be able to persuade Bee.'

'Well, I'll write to her and suggest that we do, and I'll expect to see you both next week unless I hear otherwise?' Shapiro nodded but I could see the doubt in his face.

I didn't feel very confident that they'd be back the following week. I'd come to the conclusion that their reluctance to get settled in a deeper psychotherapy was linked to their anxiety about opening up painful feelings that made them feel vulnerable, but I hoped my session with Shapiro would have reduced his anxiety and raised his curiosity enough to enable him to persuade her to come back.

I was wrong.

I received a brief email response from Bina saying thank you, but they didn't feel any more sessions would be useful. She didn't add the heart.

It was nearly a year later when I received the following email from Shapiro:

> *Hi Susanna,*
>
> *Hope you're well? Bee and I wondered if you might have time to see us again for a session? Bee's pregnant and would like to discuss a couple of issues with you.*
>
> *Cheers,*
> *Shappy*

I actually didn't have any time but I wanted to see how they were getting on, so I emailed back suggesting an appointment two weeks ahead.

Hi Susanna,

Thank you so much for returning my email. Any chance we could pop in to see you this week? It's a bit urgent.

Cheers,
Shappy

I was curious and a bit concerned. I thought something quite serious must be afoot for him to make a demand like that. I emailed them back, offering to see them on Friday, a day I didn't usually see patients.

I'd pressed the buzzer to let them in some minutes earlier and I was standing outside my consulting room wondering where they'd got to when I heard Bina's voice on the stairs below.

'God, these stairs,' she groaned.

'One more floor,' Shapiro said encouragingly.

Bina was flushed and sweaty, looking quite different from the polished woman I'd encountered the previous year. She was wearing a block print kaftan and leggings; her low-heeled brown sandals showed her swollen ankles. Her hair, which was stuck to her forehead, was piled into a messy bun with a large purple clip. She looked uncomfortable and unhappy.

They sat down on the couch, drawing water from their bags and drinking deeply. Bina asked if I could open the window and Shapiro got up to do it. There was something heavy in the air; I knew something was very wrong.

'Thanks so much for seeing us today. Shall I fill you in?' Shapiro looked at Bina to confirm that he should start and she nodded dismissively without looking at him.

'OK. First, we need to tell you that the previous sessions with you hit the bullseye. Totally helpful. Both of us felt it really made a difference. Right, hon?'

Bina didn't respond.

'We started trying right after ending the sessions. First month, no luck. Second month, boom! And here we are! Baby's due in five weeks!' Shapiro looked at me expectantly but I wasn't sure what to say. It all seemed so unreal; his enthusiastic bonhomie felt deeply fake.

'But the pregnancy has been a bit tricky. Bee's been . . .' He searched for the word. 'A bit down. Maybe depressed?' He glanced furtively at Bina, who sat motionless and unresponsive.

There was a silence. I looked at Bina, hoping she'd say something herself, but her head was down and she seemed, at that moment, quite unreachable.

I waited. And waited. I sensed strongly that if I tried to quiz Bina, she'd withdraw further. She needed to feel that it was her choice to open up to me, that it was in her power to speak or not.

So I waited some more, drifting off into my own thoughts as we sat together in silence, until Bina's voice brought me back into the present. It flashed across my mind as she began to speak that my disconnection had mirrored hers.

'I don't know what you all want me to say,' Bina said flatly.

'Just explain to Susanna how you've been, how you're feeling,' Shapiro instructed and I nodded encouragingly too.

'Fat. That's how I'm feeling. Disgusting. Fat.'

It took a lot of prompting and patience for Bina to share what was going on. She'd never told anyone her feelings about her body and her struggle with eating. She said she felt gross, ugly and out of control and her old routine of restricting her diet and obsessive exercise just wasn't possible now. She was veering between starving herself and then bingeing, prompted by an aching hunger like she'd never experienced before. She felt as though she couldn't go on, that she hated herself, wanted to obliterate herself. She didn't want to live if she had to live like this.

I asked Bina, as gently as possible, if she'd thought about hurting herself or even made plans to do so.

'No. I wouldn't hurt the baby.'

She looked stricken. As though the reality of the baby had just dawned on her. I felt more present with her than I'd ever been and I had a strong impulse to get up and hug her; there was something so lonely and tragic in her voice. I'd never really seen this part of Bina before; it had been so carefully hidden behind her glossy façade. But now it felt she could, at last, acknowledge the mess she was in and the need she had to be cared for and to be understood. And in doing that, she brought me closer to her.

'It's really good you're talking to Susanna, hon,' Shapiro said, turning to me. 'I've been really worried. Bee's just not been her old self at all. I'm really glad she's told you what's been going on. What do you think Bee needs to do?'

'I'm not sure it's about *doing*, Shapiro. Maybe first it's about listening?'

'Oh, absolutely. I want to listen. But should Bina see a psychiatrist? What do you think?'

'Perhaps but let's have a bit of a think first though.'

By the end of the session, I think Shapiro felt relieved and I could see why he'd pushed to see me urgently. I suggested I should write to Bina's GP and that she might need some individual help alongside the couple work. They listened carefully. I consulted my diary and we agreed they'd come back on Wednesday at 8am; the only time I could offer.

I spoke to her doctor and emailed a colleague who specialised in eating disorders to see if she had a space for Bina and, by Wednesday, I felt I'd begun to put the care that was going to be needed around this young family.

On Wednesday, I arrived at Queen Anne Street sweaty

and thirsty; the Tube had been pulsing with the previous day's heat. There was no time to pop to the café to get a coffee and a bottle of water so I opened the windows, put out a new box of tissues, checked the bathroom for loo paper and sat down to wait.

They didn't come. They didn't phone or text. I checked my email to no avail. At 8.45am, I dashed out to the café to get my coffee and added a croissant to my order as compensation for being dicked about.

The day passed uneventfully. I checked my phone between sessions but there was nothing from either Shapiro or Bina. On the way home, I checked again and wrote a brief email to them both, hoping that everything was OK and suggesting they be in touch.

The week passed quickly and, like the pencil scribbles, my interest began to fade. I'd done my best; I'd let the GP know and I'd connected Bina up with an outstanding psychotherapist. There was nothing more I could do.

Psychotherapists often have to bear rejection. Many patients, fearful of the depth of their need, slap the offered hand away. Most times, the psychotherapist has to offer it again, and sometimes again and again and again – session after session. Bina's secret eating disorder was, in some ways, completely unsurprising. She hated her neediness so much that she fought against the reality of her body's requirement for food. She wanted to control that part of her, the hunger that left her feeling out of control. Through their response to my offers of help, I felt I'd begun to understand their fears, but understanding was useless if they wouldn't come.

It was November, nearly five months later, when I heard from them again. And once more, it was Shapiro who reached out, leaving a friendly message on my phone. There was no apology and little information, just a polite request to be seen. I mulled over whether I wanted to see them again. Was I resentful? Was it a waste of time? But my concern (and curiosity) overrode my reluctance and I offered them a Zoom session the following week. It was all I had.

A week later, I sat in my office at home and started the Zoom meeting just a minute before the session was due to begin. I looked at myself on the screen and, noting the tiredness around my eyes, I reached for the cheering lipstick on my desk. Then, ping, there they were. I could see that they were sitting on a large green velvet sofa and behind them was a striking abstract painting. Everything looked comfortable and organised and there seemed to be no sign of a baby in the view I had.

I smiled at them and commented that it was some time since we'd met. They smiled back and there was a little flurry between them whilst they decided who would start.

'Well, we have a son! Darsh. Four months!' Shapiro said, his voice slightly strained. 'It's been . . . challenging but we're doing OK, I think.' And he glanced nervously at Bina who was sitting passively beside him.

She looked drained. Her hair was glossy and down around her face but her skin looked sallow and pinched, and I could see her collarbones jutting out from the neck of her cream jumper.

'Congratulations. How have you both been?' I asked, directing my gaze at Bina.

'Not so good,' she replied. 'The birth was very tough, long. I had to have a Caesarean in the end. I was in labour for 22 hours and then they were concerned about his heart rate, so they took me in for an emergency Caesar and then I had an infection, so I haven't really done very well at breastfeeding him. I got mastitis when I got home, so they put me on antibiotics and then I had a reaction to the antibiotics, which meant I had to go back to hospital without Darsh. He's a lovely boy but he doesn't sleep so . . . I'm exhausted to be honest.' Bina spoke without pause, the words breathlessly tumbling out of her. I thought she looked shell-shocked, as though she couldn't make sense of all that had happened and was happening to her.

The rest of the session was spent unpacking all this. It seemed the pregnancy, the birth and the first months felt to Bina like a trauma. Her usual ways of managing her feelings and her body had all been thrown into disarray and she was trying hard, and failing, to find a new equilibrium.

This time there was no prevarication, no wish to limit the number of sessions. They jumped into the therapy with both feet and I was a lifeboat to a pair of drowning children. After a couple of weeks of Zoom sessions, a regular appointment at my office became available and we agreed they should come in person.

It was a truly horrid winter day. Bitterly cold, icy and dark. I didn't feel like leaving home myself so I was doubtful that Shapiro and Bina would brave the elements but at 4pm the buzzer buzzed and, moments later, Bina, wearing a baby, arrived in my office.

'Just me today, I'm afraid. Shapiro had to go up to Leeds for work. Sorry,' she said, as she unwrapped Darsh from his sling and then unwrapped herself from the many layers of clothing she was wearing to keep out the cold. She didn't mention the presence of the baby or why she'd brought him and so neither did I.

Darsh sat on her lap passively facing me, his dark shock of hair standing upright as she pulled off his woolly blue hat. He looked at me intently with large brown eyes and bunched his small fist into his mouth. I smiled at him, and he frowned.

'I thought you'd like to meet him,' Bina explained. Darsh grumbled, whimpering a little and arching his back and immediately a look of panic spread over Bina's face.

'I don't know what's the matter,' she said, frowning. 'I just fed him before we walked here.'

She pulled on his little tracksuit bottoms and said, 'No poo. Shall I feed him again?'

'Perhaps today you'd like me to take care of you *and* him?' I said.

'That'd be nice,' she responded smiling. 'I'm exhausted.'

Darsh whimpered again and his face crumpled in displeasure.

'What is it Darsh? What do you want?' Her voice was slightly despairing. 'I don't seem to ever know what he wants.' But, before she could elaborate on her thought, Darsh's grumbling descended into a full-scale complaint and he began to cry.

Bina looked stumped. She lifted Darsh up and scrambled to her feet where she stood awkwardly jiggling him up and down. It was excruciating to watch – to see how helpless Bina felt and how lost Darsh was without a mother who could soothe him. His cries grew louder and her desperation grew larger and she looked at me with such misery that I felt tears prick my eyes. It felt so pitiful, I wanted to take them both into my arms.

It goes without saying that a psychotherapist must be able to empathise with people. In that moment, as I observed the crisis that was unfolding between Darsh and Bina, I felt empathy for them both. Darsh's frantic cries pierced into me with urgent need and Bina's forlorn desperation touched me too. A baby's cry hits us in the gut. It's designed that way – we're hardwired to respond to that helplessness, an infant's survival depends on that we do. But I've also been a mother and I know how daunting that can be; how tough mothering is and how painful it is to feel helpless in the face of desperate crying.

The Italian neuroscientist Vittorio Gallese has discovered

that when we empathise with someone, identical neural systems in both brains fire up. It's as though our brain is working to replicate the feelings of another person. In these experiences of empathic identification, we connect to an emotion that we may have had in the past but which is not our own in the present. For a moment, we allow ourselves to feel the other's despair, fear, rage or joy. But if we lose ourselves in someone else's feelings, or we find those feelings too overwhelming, we can't help them – we need to fall into the feelings, connect and then separate our emotions from theirs, all in the twinkling of an eye. If we fail to empathise like this with our children or our partners, they feel misunderstood. And whilst that seems a little thing, being misunderstood by those we love is a painful, alienating experience.

That afternoon, was I witnessing Bina's trouble with empathising with Darsh? I think she knew he was uncomfortable and unhappy but it seemed she didn't feel she could help him cope with it. It wasn't that she couldn't empathise with him, it was that she felt too much like him? Desperate and helpless.

Darsh kept crying and Bina kept on jiggling. Eventually, I stood up and put out my arms to take him. He wriggled frantically and arched his back but I held him firmly against my shoulder and he began to quieten. Bina sat down and stared, her mouth slightly open, her face vacant.

'He likes you,' she said weakly.

'You must be very tired,' I said and she nodded. Darsh was quiet now and I handed him back to Bina.

'Do you mind if I feed him? Is that OK?'

She lifted her sweater and I saw Darsh shiver with excitement and root for her breast, attaching himself firmly with loud sucky noises.

'At least the feeding seems to be going better now. I

nearly gave up but the midwife said I should keep at it,' Bina said.

As Darsh sucked rhythmically, we also seemed to get into a rhythm. She talked and I listened. She told me her worries about her nipples, how she thought they were the wrong shape. How she worried that Shapiro wouldn't find her body attractive, how they hadn't even tried to have sex. She said her mother seemed fearful of helping with Darsh and she talked about how disappointed she felt about that. Her mum couldn't understand how hard she was finding it and kept suggesting she should get a nanny. But though she didn't want a nanny, she couldn't really understand why. She talked and I listened and whilst we talked, Darsh slept, unmoving at her breast.

Most of the change that therapy brings is through these ordinary conversations – week in, week out. Patients talk about their lives, couples discuss who fills the fridge, who empties the bin. If people change, become more loving, more open to each other or themselves, it's because someone has listened. Someone has listened who can bear to hear it all, the good, the bad and, indeed, the ugly.

I don't think anyone had really listened to Shapiro or Bina before; their brittle defences were the result of childhoods that hadn't provided the understanding that children need to flourish. They'd been brought up to prize achievement above everything else and they had bought into that and created a shared culture within their marriage that put feelings and relationships way down the list of priorities. But babies have a way of changing things. They pull us back to our own infancy, stirring feelings often long repressed. Babies make us remember, so that in remembering, we can listen to the messages in their cries.

Many couples pull themselves away from these feelings; mothers ignore the tingling in their breasts as their milk lets down on the way to the office. Fathers drop the baby at nursery and slog on to work to pay the bills. Most parents have no choice. Of course, sometimes it's a relief to get away from the raw needs of a child but does it also mean shutting down and disconnecting from these raw needs? How else do you hand over the most precious thing in your life to someone else, for eight or nine hours a day?

We've structured a world in which the care of children seems to come way down the list of our priorities. Governments want workers and women rightly protest the disadvantage that full-time motherhood brings. But who advocates for the baby, who advocates for the importance of parents being able to be parents? We now know how critical the early years are, how the experiences that children have between birth and three can shape all of their lives. Do long hours in nursery care provide an optimal experience for most children? Do most parents of young children want to spend more time at work than with their infants? Why can't we allow new parents to work less? Why don't we value the time they spend caring for their family as much as the time spent in the office?

As a psychotherapist, it's not my job to judge or to recommend a particular way of living. But psychotherapy is political because its manifesto values the importance of human relationships much more than money or success. It's also true to say that a good therapy often resets the values of our patients, altering their priorities.

I think the therapy with Bina and Shapiro helped them. Everything about them softened and they didn't hire the two nannies after all. Bina never went back to her old job and when Darsh was one, Shapiro left his job too. They wanted a different future for themselves and something different to their own childhoods for Darsh. By the time they finished the therapy, Bina was pregnant again and they'd started their own business and this time, it was going to be a family business.

GABRIELLE AND JOHANNES BLOW THE STRAW HOUSE DOWN AND THEN DO SOME REBUILDING

I'm dreaming about a boat. It sails, tacking back and forth in the gentlest of winds, luffing more than actually moving. The boat is a sickly yellow and I'm trying desperately to steer it through rock-strewn waters. I'm scared I'm going to run aground and there's a nagging worry about what's below deck and whether it can get out. Is there a hole in the hull? Then I wake, sweating, my nose dry and my throat raw.

It was my fifth day of being ill. The coronavirus had come on suddenly. I'd cooked lunch for friends and we'd had the back door open in celebration of spring, which was just poking its nose through the grey, wet weather. It was convivial; we'd bumped elbows and reassured each other that we'd still have a summer. Plans were made for meeting in Suffolk as we drank our way through a long, lazy lunch. Later, I felt hot. 'I've got that coronavirus thing,' I told my husband. He scoffed but frowned when I showed him the thermometer.

I'd upgraded my Zoom account the previous week – it was obvious that trotting off to Queen Anne Street to see my patients wasn't going to be sustainable. We'd bought the hand sanitiser and I'd taken to wiping down the doorknobs between sessions but by mid-March the virus had got out of the pen and was rampaging through central London. There were conversations amongst my colleagues about Zoom,

Skype and Microsoft Teams, and hastily convened meetings to share know-how and concerns about moving – sometimes very vulnerable patients – online. And then I became ill and my patients had to wait.

Two weeks later, I was sufficiently recovered to restart my practice in this new and rather unsettling world. I'd taken care to buy myself a new camera to upgrade the one on my old laptop and I'd rearranged my home office with an easy chair from my downstairs consulting room. I placed the laptop on my office chair so I could adjust the height and strapped myself into Zoom. It felt very strange and, still exhausted from the virus, I wasn't looking forward to the day.

I was due to see Johannes and Gabrielle, who consulted me from time to time. When they first came, acrimony and distrust suffused every word they spoke. Back then, I had needed all my authority to quell the accusations and counter-accusations that were being flung about my office like grenades. They'd been in and out of court for a year and the judge, fed up with them, had wearily suggested they seek therapy. Neither wanted to be sitting with each other in my consulting room but they'd run out of road with their fantasy that they could win the battle and avoid compromise. Gradually, they'd made progress and been able to co-operate a little more around their two children. But the peace was fragile and when it broke down, they came to see me.

Both of them were fat. Not nicely rounded in a way that suggested just one too many trips to the fridge but so overweight that it seemed to suggest a sustained refusal to care for themselves. Was something desperate and destructive being expressed through their bodies, which was echoed in the anger that they vented on each other?

I like parenting consultations – they're different from long, ongoing psychotherapy. I enjoy the work with couples who are finding it hard to adjust to being parents or who are suddenly really challenged by an adolescent revolt. I find satisfaction in supporting parents who are worried because their child is depressed, school refusing or in other kinds of trouble. I like it because I can use different parts of myself – I can be a kind of parenting coach; I can be a sympathetic ear; I can offer some reflections on the family dynamics and I can relate to parents from my own experience of parenting. Most important of all, I feel that I'm caring for the children too.

Every couple therapist is confronted with the challenges children present to a relationship and many couples who seek therapy argue a lot about parenting. What is clear from numerous studies across the globe is that marital satisfaction declines steeply when you have a baby. Google 'marital satisfaction and having children' and you will see a plethora of graphs showing a U-shaped curve. Happiness declines with the first child and having further children makes the decline deeper. Then, just as things seem to be getting easier, children reach the teenage years and couple contentment goes into a further deep dive. But stick it out because as the children begin to leave home, things gradually improve. I remember years ago showing these graphs during a training day for children's centre managers and there was a shocked silence until one woman stood up in dismay, blurting, 'Why did no one tell me this?!'

This decline in relationship happiness frequently begins in the first year after the birth of a baby. The baby arrives and, for most couples, there is joy – grandparents coo, friends bring cakes, balloons, cards and flowers arrive with the postman and everything is mostly rosy for a while. But baby coming first eventually takes its toll and as time passes, parents come to realise that their needs have been overtaken by their children's, which can evoke strong feelings of deprivation and neglect. These feelings may reactivate distress about similar feelings experienced earlier in their lives, adding an overlay from the past to the intensity of what is happening in the present. In response to these feelings, each partner may look to the other to fill the gap and to ameliorate these feelings of deprivation, which then provokes a competition of needs. Couples begin to argue about whose turn it is to change a nappy, whose turn is it to get up in the night or whose turn it is to have a night out with friends. In this situation, parents begin to 'shift parent', monitoring who's clocked on and who's having time off. Whilst this seems to be a kind of solution to the arguments, in time, this kind of parenting produces even further distance between the couple and pleasures derived from shared activities around the children are lost.

The experience of mothers is often somewhat different from fathers. Mothers still undertake a greater proportion of domestic and child-rearing tasks than men, though there is evidence that this is beginning to change. Men often feel something of the outsider in the face of the intense breastfeeding dyad of mother and baby and this sense of exclusion leads some men to focus on their life outside the family, which in practice often means their work. On the other hand, rather than feeling excluded, mothers may have strong claustrophobic feelings as they spend all day with an infant in their arms or at their breast. These differing experiences can make having sex tricky. Men want sex to reclaim their partners, to reassure and be reassured that there is still time for adult love amid the love fest around the baby. But women may find their strongest urge is not for more cuddles but for more space and their partner's wish for sex may be felt as a further encroachment on themselves.

And then there are the in-laws. Up until a baby comes, the couple may have chosen to be quite insular from the wider family but suddenly grandparents and aunts and uncles appear. They may be helpful, and they certainly may be needed, but a renewed connection between one partner and their family of origin may require big adjustments and the need to redraw the boundaries around the relationship. Family culture – how you parent, make a Christmas, make a home and celebrate birthdays – is often derived from what we experienced in our own childhood. A new family has to work out what its new culture will be and this negotiation can bring about conflict when expectations of family life differ. Grandma and Mummy may have one view about how baby should be fed that may differ hugely from Daddy's expectations derived from his own family.

All the challenges I describe above can be usefully explored in couple therapy and it is a great shame that couples often leave it far too long to come and talk about these matters. Over recent years, successive governments have placed greater emphasis on early intervention for new parents, initiating pilot schemes to encourage them to focus on their relationship and as a result, some years ago, I and a colleague set up a co-parenting consultation service.

We expected concerned and anxious parents of teenage children and younger parents struggling with their babies and with collaborating over sleep training, feeding and childcare. To our surprise, none of these couples came. Instead, we saw broken couples who really didn't want to co-operate, who'd much prefer it if their ex was dead or gone. We had lawyers sending us huge files containing the miserable details of bitter disputes. We had couples who literally wouldn't sit together in the consulting room and, in one case, a woman insisting her scary-looking mother be present to 'protect' her from her ex.

This all came as a shock and we were, initially, quite unprepared. Gradually, however, we learnt to work with these separated couples and were often able to help. We were also naively shocked at how little provision there is for these parents who fall outside of the court system. How little, as a society, we have concerned ourselves with the plight of children caught between warring parents. Every study of separation and divorce concludes that unresolved and sustained conflict between parents is deeply harmful to children and yet extraordinarily little time and few resources are made available to help these families. Lawyers make money, judges make judgements and children are left to navigate that most complex territory of managing the relationship between combatant parents. Something I, after 35 years of working with couples, can barely manage myself.

This kind of therapeutic work is often challenging and frustrating. Parents suddenly refuse to come to the sessions or they walk out midway. The therapist is copied in to email trails that list past slights and abuses. Accusations are made that can make your hair stand on end and sometimes demand a call to the GP or a social worker. And this was the case with Johannes and Gabrielle.

They had two children who were the subject of their dispute. Nathan, aged four, who, just months before they separated, had been diagnosed as autistic, and Mia, who was 20 months. I never saw their children and, at first, neither Nathan nor Mia were talked about in any real way. The children were constantly referred to but it took a long time to get a picture of how they were doing. It felt, at times, that they were just commodities to be fought over.

The first session was a nightmare. They arrived separately. Gabrielle came first and objected to being asked to wait outside until Johannes arrived. I knew it would be fatal to begin without him; I didn't want to start by creating any sense that she and I had established some rapport from which he was excluded. But at the time, I had no waiting room and it was a bitterly cold day outside. The minutes ticked by and

I felt worse and worse for leaving Gabrielle in the street. Eventually, I heard footsteps and both tumbled down the stairs and into my office in a rush. I was startled by their size. They seemed to take up a lot of space and I suddenly felt a bit overwhelmed by their presence.

'Shall we begin?' I asked, as they settled in the two chairs that were furthest apart.

Gabrielle shot me a hostile look and then, ignoring Johannes, said, 'Why the fuck is he so late?' Without waiting for an answer, she proceeded to tell me that it was pointless being here and that she was only doing it because her court appointed social worker said she must. She then added that I mustn't believe anything Johannes said as he was a patho-logical liar.

This wasn't a promising start. And worse, within min-utes, the two of them were in meltdown and I was just an observer as Johannes accused Gabrielle of deliberately mis-leading him about the time of the appointment.

I put up my hand, palm flat and outwards, and firmly told them that if they wanted to spend their money on this argument they certainly could but it was a pointless waste and, more importantly, wouldn't in any way help their chil-dren. I can't say that this was a turning point. In that first session, I must have raised my hand to stop them half a dozen times. But when I asked them to tell me about Nathan and Mia, when I enquired about Mia's language development and how they felt about Nathan's diagnosis of autism, they grew slightly more circumspect, at least for a while.

Four days after the first session, I had an email from Johannes saying that his contact with the children had been stopped because Gabrielle had accused him of being 'inappro-priate' with Nathan. My heart sank, this was deeply worrying. I learnt that Nathan had apparently told his mother that he'd 'played with' Daddy's penis in the bath and now social workers were investigating. Johannes was outraged, asserting that nothing had occurred beyond a four-year-old's ordinary curiosity. I wasn't surprised when they cancelled their session.

Separating is hard; losing love and that sense of belonging to someone is disorientating and painful. Often, we erect such enormous barriers to mourning our losses that it can seem impossible to see over the top of them, towards a future. Some people mourn quietly; they retreat and hide themselves away. Others mourn a separation noisily, sharing their grief, their hurt and their worries with friends, therapists, colleagues and family. Many of us mourn angrily. We find ourselves furious at our losses, raging at the unfairness of it and incensed by the sense of powerlessness that loss engenders. And, furious, we look to blame and punish, which is a potent recipe for a court battle.

Two months later, the couple asked for a further appointment. Johannes had emailed to tell me that an investigation had been conducted and social services reported no concerns. The children were able to resume their overnight stays with him but, he wrote, Gabrielle was still putting up barriers in the way of his contact with the children. I agreed to see them the following week, prepared for the session to be difficult.

Within minutes of arriving, Johannes broke down in angry tears as he described the child welfare investigation and the intrusion and the shame. He told me how scared he'd been, how fearful he was. Would he be charged with abuse? Would he lose the children? For over a month, he had no contact with either of the children and then he'd only been able to see them at a contact centre whilst a social worker observed him. As he spoke, Gabrielle sat there listening, seemingly chastened. But her silence didn't last and it wasn't long before they, hot with feeling, began to fight. Again, I focused relentlessly on how their children were being damaged by this fighting and it seemed, slowly, to be sinking in.

'I know you really want to hurt each other, to pay each other back for the pain and distress you feel, but you need to realise there's no such thing as a clean, clear shot here. There's always collateral damage. Your children are getting hit by the shrapnel from your fights every day.'

During this early period, I had several single sessions with them. I knew they were both still deeply wounded from what had occurred in their relationship and how it had ended and I believed these residual feelings were getting in the way of their parenting. They had told me that their relationship had always been intense, passionate and stormy and, though they were both resolved it was over, they were certainly having a hard time moving on. It seemed to me that they kept the previous intensity of their old relationship going by having these endless fights and even though they were now separated, they seemed to be just as involved with each other through these rows as they'd been when they were together. Were these fights a way of avoiding a real ending? Perhaps this lively combat was better than being faced with the desolate silence of mourning?

Johannes, a writer of crime fiction, was a curious mix. He spoke fluently with a confident assurance that came from his stellar education and his career success and yet, despite his imposing size and voice, he conveyed an anxious vulnerability too. His mother had put him temporarily into care when he was a toddler, which led to periods with foster parents and stays in children's homes. He would see his mother from time to time but she never seemed able to provide a permanent home for him, so, eventually, aged six, he was adopted. His adoptive parents, he told me, were loving but they were members of an evangelical church which meant that life was rather austere and very rule bound. Now, he hated rules or rigidity of any sort and, though he was reeling from losing his home and terrified that Gabrielle would take the children from him, he found it hard to go along with all the rules about when and how he could see them. Johannes had a quick intelligence and saw immediately when I pointed it out that the abandonment he'd experienced in his early childhood and the rigidity of his adoptive parents were affecting his responses to the current situation. But though he knew this intellectually, deep in his gut he felt an overwhelming sense of distrust and fear.

Whilst Johannes wore his heart on his sleeve, Gabrielle was much more closed. Her grief was locked up inside her and she regarded me not as an ally but as someone who was judging her. She was startlingly pretty. Her rounded face had a luminous quality, with clear olive skin and rich dark brown straight hair. She spoke with a strong South African accent and often turned her face away from me, which combined to make me feel both dismissed and curious about her. Later, I began to see that she turned away to hide her feelings and that great shame was attached to any expression of vulnerability. She said little about her childhood except that her parents had divorced when she was four and that her mother had remarried a bullying, selfish man whom Gabrielle had hated. Her stepfather had died when she was 19 and Gabrielle's indifference to his death had driven a permanent wedge between her and her mother.

It took nearly a year of fortnightly and then monthly sessions before things were calmer. And then, with some general agreements in place about care of the children and money issues, they ended therapy on the understanding they could come and see me from time to time if they wished. And they did. Every six months or so, they'd come and we'd discuss issues they were struggling with. Which nursery for Mia? What help for Nathan? Could Johannes's new girlfriend meet the children?

When working with separated couples, I often think of the 'Judgement of Solomon', a story from the Old Testament in which King Solomon of Israel rules between two women, both claiming to be the mother of a child. Unable to agree, Solomon tells the mothers that the solution is to cut the child in two, so that each of them can have a half. A sword is brought to the King to enact his judgement and then the real mother, unable to bear her son being killed, offers the child to the other woman to save the baby's life, whilst the other agrees to the halving. In this way the false mother is exposed and King Solomon then restores the child to its real mother. Sometimes, in the work with Johannes and Gabrielle, I felt as if I was being asked to be a kind of Solomon, though I never recommended any chopping up of either Nathan or Mia!

I was proud of Johannes and Gabrielle and proud of my work. They might still squabble and cuss but, in the end, they'd decided not to damage their babies but to put them first, even if it meant at times giving in to each other.

But as lockdown kicked in, here they were again, arguing fiercely from the trenches of their respective living rooms. I wondered if Zoom was making it easier for them to let rip, that they felt safer chucking accusations via a computer rather than in person. It was as if all the work we'd done over the years now counted for nothing. I wondered if this was the result of three weeks of lockdown – schools and nurseries were closed and they were now both on their own with the children. Johannes looked desperate and his sense of desperation began to infect me as the intermittent message *Johannes's internet is unstable* was accompanied by the loss of sound and vision. My head hurt as I tried to gather up what was going on but it was impossible to make much sense because I could only hear one word in three.

'Susanna, can you hear me? Susanna, can I speak?'

Gabrielle interrupted. 'Why is your internet so shit Johannes? Can't you do something about it? Turn off your video.'

Eventually, I learnt that the dispute was over where the children should reside during lockdown. Nathan and Mia were currently at Gabrielle's in Hackney but, as the pandemic had hit, Johannes had fled from his flat by Victoria Park to his girlfriend's cottage in Sussex. Gabrielle was adamant that the children shouldn't travel to the countryside, that it was against the rules and wasn't safe. If Johannes wanted to see them, he should come back to London.

'There's no way they're going to Sussex. It's not safe and I don't want them that far from me. What if they're ill? And actually, what if I get ill when they're with me? I didn't even know that he wasn't at home until I called him on Tuesday with a migraine and he said he couldn't come and pick them up. So, Susanna, I was left with them on my own, thinking I was going to be really ill with coronavirus. It's such a complete betrayal of my trust . . . as usual, you're just putting yourself first.' She would have continued but I stopped her in mid-sentence.

'Johannes, I'm unclear why you're in Sussex?' I asked, hoping he could hear me across the flickering screen.

'I needed to be with Liz.'

'What the fuck does that mean?' Gabrielle interrupted. 'Why? Why do you need to be with her and not your children?'

There was a silence.

'Are you still there, Johannes?' I asked.

'Yes, yes, I'm here. Look, Gabs, it seems obvious to get the kids out of London – London is where all the virus is. I think they would be safer here with me. It's only for a few weeks, you don't even have a garden and here they can have lots of space and enjoy the weather—'

A storm erupted at these words – one that overtook the rest of the session and that I couldn't calm. Both were angry. Johannes believed that Gabrielle was deliberately misunderstanding his intentions, whilst she was incandescent and, I suspected, very fearful that he would somehow win this argument. The only good thing that came from the session was the agreement to have another session three days later.

Things were calmer when we Zoomed again. Johannes had driven back to London after the previous session and for the last two nights the children had been with him at his London flat. They were now watching TV in the next room whilst I tried to help their parents come to some agreement about their care.

'Gabs, it just doesn't make any sense for me to stay in London *or* for the children to. Liz has a lovely cottage, not far from the sea; they've got their own rooms and it's much more sensible for the children. *And* safer. If you were putting the children first, and thinking about what was best for them, you'd be happy for them to go.'

He went on in this vein for several minutes and, despite the reasonableness of his tone, I could see that Gabrielle was getting more and more distressed at the thought of her children ensconced in this dream cottage with Johannes and Liz.

Her voice was clipped and deliberate when she spoke. 'J, you know, I've known you forever. This isn't about the children – you know it and I know it.' Then she addressed me. 'It's because he can't be away from his bloody girlfriend. And that's fine but we're in the middle of a fucking pandemic for fuck's sake. Can't you just do without your daily fuck for a few weeks?!'

The next few minutes were a storm of accusations and insults as they shouted and bitched at each other like in the bad old days – the intensity of their anger seemed greater than ever, as though the screen protected them and they could really let rip. I leant forward into the camera. 'OK. OK! Let's just calm down. Johannes! Gabrielle! Please!' But Gabrielle was in full flight and wouldn't be stopped.

I felt helpless. If they'd been in the room with me, I would, I knew, be able to shut them up. The force of my authority and their sense of propriety would have brought some order but here on Zoom, I just couldn't get through. I sat back in my chair, defeated.

'And if I get ill, who'll look after the children? Who's going to help me with the children if you've swanned off to Suffolk with her?'

'Not Suffolk! Sussex! Are you deaf as well as stupid?'

And it went around and around. All my usual compromises weren't, in this situation, going to work. The Covid restrictions forbade travelling but Johannes was determined to go back to Sussex the following day and he continued to threaten to take the children with him. We were getting nowhere and I found myself uncertain about what was best. Everyone knew that London was at the epicentre of the coronavirus and was Gabrielle's small, gardenless flat going to be the best option? Perhaps they *would* be better off in the countryside? I could see that the rural idyll he was describing could be good for the children but I also knew that Mia and Nathan would find it very difficult to be separated from their mother for weeks on end. I felt torn and I still couldn't quite understand why Johannes was so determined to break lockdown to go to Liz's.

The session ended with a tenuous agreement from Johannes that he would stay put for the next week but he wouldn't give any assurances beyond that.

It was a long day of Zoom sessions before I finally shut my laptop to head downstairs to make dinner. I was pouring myself a large gin and tonic when my phone dinged – it was a text from Johannes.

Hi Susanna, sorry to bother you but could I call you tomorrow? I HAVE to get back to Sussex – Liz is five months pregnant and not doing very well. I need to find a way to be straight about it with Gabs. J

Now it made sense. I put on some water for the pasta and peeled onions and thought about what to do next. Both Johannes and Gabrielle had their fragilities and were easily triggered by fears of losing the children and being controlled by each other. It was a toxic mix of feelings that produced storms of overwhelming emotion, where neither could think calmly. A new baby in the middle of a pandemic wasn't going to make things any easier. Gabrielle was going to test Johannes on his loyalty to her and the children; the danger was that, rather than reassuring her, he would feel oppressed by this and get angry. Gabrielle's own childhood was also likely to compound the already tense situation, I knew she liked Liz but the idea of her children now being part of a brand new family, from which she was excluded, was going to echo her own experience and make it hard for her to cope with. As I crushed garlic and sipped my drink, I began to feel quite pessimistic that they'd get through lockdown without another falling-out.

New partners and new babies are extremely challenging events for separated parents, activating competitive feeling states that can make empathy and concern almost impossible. As infants, we are hardwired to protest when there is any potential threat that might come between us and our parent, and that protest is often louder when a child already has a feeling of insecurity. That's why children nearly always have ambivalent feelings when a new sibling arrives, uncertain whether this is a delightful new playmate or someone who will steal the food of parental love from their mouths. Human parenting is equally instinctive, often driven by biological impulses. If we feel our children are threatened or our connection to them is at risk, we react strongly. If our own childhood was insecure, we may be particularly alert to these threats and when we feel there is jeopardy, our emotional responses may be more reactive than considered. I knew all this but how would I help Gabrielle and Johannes through this storm?

I feared they would fight as if their lives depended on it. Gabrielle would hold the children close and Johannes would react to this by becoming controlling and aggressive, which would then confirm Gabrielle's worst fears. I'd seen them play out this dynamic on numerous occasions and here it was again. They were gridlocked in lockdown and it was going to take time and work to unlock all these entangled feelings.

I was having trouble with my back and I blamed Zoom. There was something about staring into a screen that was creating problems in my neck, probably because I was constantly craning forward to get closer to my patients. Sessions with Johannes and Gabrielle had continued intermittently through the early summer and I felt grumbly and frustrated with how regressed they both seemed – petty and vindictive. Gabrielle had taken Liz's pregnancy quite well on the surface but now a row had broken out about whether Nathan should start school in September or not.

'Nathan won't cope with starting school under these circumstances; it's selfish of you to want to send him. Once again, Gabs, this is all about you and what you want and not about him. How is a little boy with his needs going to cope with teachers in masks and parents who aren't allowed into the school? The whole thing is fucking ridiculous.' Johannes was on a roll and I raised a hand and my voice to stop him.

'You don't believe in him anymore,' Gabrielle said, shaking her head in disgust. 'You're treating him with no respect. He wants to go. He's been looking forward to this for a long,

long time. I, I . . .' she struggled for words. 'I think you've written him off, as though because he's autistic it doesn't really matter if he goes to school at all. I've sorted everything out. Got Islington to ensure he's got a helper; spoken to his class teacher; Zoomed the head three times. What the fuck have you done? And now, you want to stop him going . . . Fuck YOU!'

It went on like this, session after session. Moments of accord wouldn't hold and I feared that they were heading back to court – though over what exactly wasn't clear. Then, two weeks later, there was a breakthrough. And it was all down to Mia.

They'd been doing a handover of the children in Highgate Wood and they'd begun to argue. Meanwhile, Mia had fallen over in the toddler playground. Neither of them noticed and another parent had picked her up and, unaware of who she belonged to, carried her crying and bleeding to the café to find the park keepers. Finally noticing Mia had vanished, Johannes and Gabrielle had become frantic and ran about the woods dragging Nathan with them. By the time they located her, Mia was in such a state that it took hours to soothe her. And now Mia, who'd recently come out of nappies, had regressed and was peeing and pooing her pants, which alarmed them both.

'I can see you both still feel very shocked and upset. It must have been dreadful. Really frightening.' Shame and guilt animated their faces but I didn't want to name it. I wanted them to.

They both nodded. And it was silent for some time. Then Gabrielle spoke.

'It's got to stop. I know we've got to stop. I don't want to hurt the kids. That's why I've kept agreeing to sessions with you, Susanna. Look Jo, whatever you want. If you don't want Nathan to start in September. Fine. Whatever. We just *have* to be on the same page. I can't go on with these arguments anymore. It's killing me and we're letting them down.'

I saw then that Johannes looked tearful and tormented. And then *I* felt tearful. Gabrielle had moved me; her passion and regret seeped through Zoom and right into my body. Then Johannes began to speak, slowly, haltingly.

'It's not been you, Gabs; it's been . . . mostly me. I've been angry with you. Fucked up about Nathan. And about us. About leaving. I'm sorry. I'm sorry.'

And then both of them were crying.

'You've both been feeling so guilty about the break-up for so long,' I began, 'and it's been painful to own this guilt. Perhaps because it stems, I think, from a feeling that you've done something very destructive by separating. And then you've both tried to get rid of that awful feeling of guilt by pushing it away and forcing the blame onto each other. Perhaps now it can stop? Perhaps now you can try to bear your own guilt. Own it, work it through and stop blaming.' I paused. 'If you don't, then the feelings of guilt will escalate because the anger between you creates a sense that you *are* destructive. The anger makes you, as we've just been hearing, forget the children's needs. Guilt, anger, blame. Guilt, anger, blame. It's a cycle – and I think you're ready to make it stop.'

I was quiet then and they were quiet, and it felt, for the first time in a long time, peaceful.

KELLY ANNE BECOMES A WICKED STEPMOTHER

In those early weeks of the first lockdown, every Zoom session confirmed how anxious people were. Even those who said they felt a new kind of freedom away from work, sequestered at home, seemed to me to be somehow disconnected from reality. One man, who said he was 'loving lockdown', dreamt he was riding a horse – but its legs came off and he found himself stuck in quicksand. Another patient dreamt of an oven that was frozen inside. And I, still disturbed by my illness, also felt disconnected and confused. All my moorings were gone and I felt I couldn't connect with my patients across the wavering, uncertain screen. And then along came Darryl and Kelly Anne.

A central tenet of being a couple therapist is even-handedness and I work hard to manage that tension and to avoid coming down on one side or another. This balance is essential to build trust and I've long learnt that although it can look like one partner is much more to blame for the troubles, in reality, couples 'cook up' their misery together. But when it came to Darryl and Kelly Anne, I not only found myself taking sides but also acting as jury, judge and executioner.

They requested an appointment just as the first lockdown was coming to an end and I postponed beginning with them until early July so I could meet them face to face, back in my central London consulting room. I made extensive preparations, bought disinfectant sprays and gels and shifted the furniture about to get the two-metre distance. Despite now being in possession of coronavirus antibodies, I was returning to Queen Anne Street with some trepidation.

Kelly Anne was in her late twenties. She spoke with a strong American twang and was pretty in a slightly plastic, shiny kind of way with short auburn hair and a deep tan. Darryl, in his mid-forties with overgrown, ginger curls and a sandy freckled complexion, spoke in a soft Scottish accent; if it hadn't been for the wild, lockdown hair, he would have been very handsome. After many weeks of Zoom meetings, it was striking what an impact being body to body in my office felt like. I felt suddenly more alive than I had for months and delighted to be meeting a couple in person.

They'd been introduced to each other just over two years ago by a rather exclusive dating agency, set up to service the wealthy in search of love. Their first date took them to Heston Blumenthal's exclusive restaurant at the Mandarin Oriental in Knightsbridge and that glamorous evening was followed by expensive trips to Paris, Barbados and New York. Both were bruised from failed relationships and they quickly sought comfort from each other and confirmation that their ex-partners were brutes and bullies.

This was Darryl's third marriage. First to Abiba, who now lived in South Africa with their 20-year-old son, and more recently to Breda, with whom he'd had two daughters, Natalie who was eleven and Catherine, eight. In that first consultation, they recounted how awful and mad Breda was and how she was a 'very bad mother'. Darryl, Kelly Anne explained, had been subject to Breda's erratic and controlling behaviour for years and, eventually, he'd cracked two years ago and left. It was clear from his stumbling account that he'd found the divorce and financial settlement brutal and, I thought, he was still deeply preoccupied and scarred by the experience.

Then Kelly Anne told me her story, which had many echoes of Darryl's. She'd been in a relationship with Kyle for three years and, from her graphic account, this man had been a bully, a cheat and a liar.

'I can't imagine how Kelly Anne stayed with that man for that long,' Darryl told me, taking over her narrative. 'Frankly, he robbed her blind, refused to leave her apartment and stole her car.'

It appeared that when they'd met, Kelly Anne had been in serious financial difficulties and Darryl had come to the rescue, employing, on her behalf, the best legal team to extricate her ex-partner from her life and her apartment as swiftly as possible. As he spoke, I got a strong sense of how important it was to Darryl that he felt himself to be a kind of hero. I said that it sounded like he'd been a knight in shining armour for Kelly Anne and they both giggled – I could see that this idea appealed to them.

They'd bonded over their difficulties, sharing their outrage at the legal shenanigans of their respective exes. Darryl's decree absolute had arrived in July, and they wasted no time planning for their wedding. They'd married late summer at the Villa Cimbrone in Ravello, a place I knew fleetingly from my own travels to be both wildly romantic and wildly expensive.

As the minutes ticked past, I began to wonder why they'd come. Everything I was hearing seemed to suggest that whilst their previous partners had been the source of much trouble for them, *they* were golden. And they'd been married less than a year.

Kelly Anne looked at Darryl. 'Tell her why we've come – you explain,' she instructed. He lifted his hands and spread them in a gesture of helplessness and resignation.

'Well, you know, er, what with lockdown and everything, my wife, I mean my ex-wife, wasn't coping er . . . so, er . . . well, she said that er . . . Natalie and Cathy needed to come and stay with us . . .' He paused and glanced anxiously at Kelly Anne. 'And, erm . . . Kelly Anne felt that Cathy was fine but Natalie . . .'

He ground to a halt and Kelly Anne shot him an angry look. 'It wasn't me who said that. I *didn't* say she couldn't come. She doesn't *want* to come. She hates me!' she concluded emphatically.

I had a sense, then, of where the problem was and how tricky this was going to be. Darryl flinched at Kelly Anne's tone and looked down, waiting for her to finish.

'She hates you?' I asked, picking up her last words and hoping to hear more. But both were quiet now and I felt they were telling me that this topic was just too dangerous to explore.

'I can see this is very distressing to talk about. It's hard to come up against such a difficulty between you, so soon after getting married.'

Both nodded but somehow the rest of the session passed without any further discussion of Darryl's daughters and soon they were leaving my office and I was still none the wiser.

It was late July before I saw them again, I'd taken a much-needed short break in Cornwall. Despite the crowds let loose from lockdown, it was revitalising and I returned to Queen Anne Street with a growing sense that things were getting back to normal. Most of my patients, however, were still on Zoom, reluctant to make the journey into central London, so I looked forward to having an in-person session with Darryl and Kelly Anne – it would be a welcome change.

They arrived with a great flurry. Kelly Anne had been shopping and was toting several chic, glossy carrier bags, which Darryl relieved her of, placing them like a barrier on the carpet between us. They looked uncomfortable on my plastic-covered sofa and I noticed they'd sat further apart from each other today. After some chit-chat they fell silent but it took only a gentle prompting from me for them to pour out the bitter and disappointed feelings that had emerged between them. I've worked with many blended families before so it was no surprise to me that the children and Kelly Anne were struggling to build a relationship, but it was a shock to hear the way Kelly Anne talked about Natalie, a girl of just 11 who was, no doubt, still coming to terms with her parents' divorce. It was very hard not to feel judgemental.

In most families, alliances shift and change as the years pass. Brothers and sisters who were close in young childhood find themselves at odds in the teenage years; fathers and sons who were best pals find themselves competing for attention and power. These changes are natural and normal, though often painful, but they come about because of ordinary processes of development within the individuals in the family, as each matures and experiments with new identities. But divorce disrupts these processes and blended families even more so.

'She doesn't like me and I don't like her,' she said in a clipped, defensive tone. 'I won't be treated with disrespect – it's not fair on me. And Darryl knows it. I don't want her coming round, giving me those sly looks and trying to get her daddy on her side. She's got to learn that things have changed. She can't have everything her own way.' Kelly Anne, now in full flow, enumerated all the terrible slights that young Natalie had inflicted on her. She'd never worn the dress that Kelly Anne had bought her; she didn't help the maid carry the dishes through to the kitchen. And so it went on . . . and on.

'The trouble is, she can twist Darryl round her little finger and he just never says no. I see her manipulating you, honey. You can't see it but I can! And I don't understand why you let her dress like that! Breda doesn't teach her that you just can't wear a dirty crop top and some torn old leggings out to dinner. I do feel quite sorry for Natalie, it's not all her fault. If no one tells her how to behave then it's no surprise she's so spoilt.'

I expected Darryl to remonstrate with her, to defend his little girl and explain her vulnerability to Kelly Anne. But he didn't, and he seemed more concerned to pacify Kelly Anne, joining her in her criticism of Natalie.

'Don't blame me, darling. I know she's difficult. *I* have as much trouble with her as you. She *is* very ungrateful. She's very like her mother and no one can expect you to make it right – but, darling, it's really not fair to blame me and if you say we can't have Natalie over then Breda won't allow poor Cathy to come and we want Cathy to come, don't we sweetie?'

As I listened to this, my mind went to a piece of research that I had heard several years before at a lecture by two brilliant, married American psychologists, Philip and Carolyn Cowan, both professors at the University of California, Berkeley. In their research, they'd noticed that where a couple were unhappy together, fathers seemed less close to their daughters. The implications were that fathers' negative feelings about their wives spilled into their relationship with their daughters, as though fathers confused these two relationships in their minds. Was this what was going on with Darryl? Was this why he seemed so down on Natalie?

As they left, I palmed my face; I felt a strong sense of distaste. This couple seemed so unfeeling and self-centred, and I felt no inclination at all to ask myself why they were like this. I only wanted to protect poor Natalie. They were due to come back next week and I felt relieved that I'd have time to consult with colleagues. I knew I needed help if I was going to be able to work with them.

But I didn't have time to speak to colleagues. Later that day, I picked up the phone to Kelly Anne who was on the other end, sobbing and screaming simultaneously. I managed to glean through the tears that Darryl had left her and gone back to Breda. She was hysterical and desperate. What should she do? They'd had a big fight, they'd thrown things, she'd pushed him and then walked out, and when she came back home an hour later, he'd left.

'Why do you think he's at Breda's, Kelly Anne?' I asked and was met with a wail. She didn't know for sure he was, she'd just assumed. So I suggested to her that perhaps he wasn't with Breda but simply licking his wounds somewhere. I told her I would see her next week, attempting to instil some sense of a boundary and calm.

But it was to no avail. I was bombarded by calls and texts all weekend, with Darryl now joining in to tell me his side of the story. He hadn't gone to Breda at all, he'd been in a hotel around the corner from where they lived in St John's Wood. She'd attacked him. She'd broken his heart. I could see how hard they were working to have me take sides and, truthfully, I still felt more on his side than hers. Anyone who spoke about an 11-year-old like that must be to blame. I felt caught in the middle between them, so I sent them a joint email and then determined not to respond to any more texts or calls.

Dear Darryl and Kelly Anne,

I'm sorry you've been having a difficult time. I will see you at 2.15pm on Tuesday when we can think together about the situation.

Best wishes,
Susanna

I was thinking about Kelly Anne and Darryl as I walked

down Marylebone High Street on the Tuesday, reflecting on
my own feelings about them, as all psychoanalytic therapists
are trained to do. I knew intellectually that the emotions
they stirred up in me could probably help me better understand their inner worlds but I couldn't get beyond feeling
simply irritated and dismissive. I felt a particular distaste for
Kelly Anne. How could she be so rejecting of this little girl?
There was something unnatural in her lack of maternal feeling for this child. Then I thought how judgemental I was
being and how little I really knew about Kelly Anne. Or Darryl, for that matter. Why *should* Kelly Anne particularly like
Natalie? Did I expect her, because she was a woman, to be
particularly nurturing? Was my judgement infected by a gen-
der bias?

Musing on this, I realised that their whole thing seemed
to be all about taking sides; all about goodies and baddies.
Cathy was good. Natalie was bad. Their exes were both clearly
unbelievably bad and apparently completely to blame for
everything that had gone wrong in their previous relationships.
And when it came to them, the same kind of black-and-white,
polarised mindset was evident. One minute, Darryl and Kelly
Anne were in idealised bliss, then the next it was all over and
they were in hell. Was *I* also guilty of taking sides? I seemed
to be treating Darryl as though he was the long-suffering
goody, doing his best, whilst I felt Kelly Anne behaved just
like a spoilt child.

This kind of splitting into good and bad was something
I'd encountered many times before and I knew that behind
this way of being, there was probably a lot of suffering inside
both of them. As I reached Queen Anne Street, I didn't like
them any better but I'd begun to become a little more curious about them. It would have to do.

They seemed a little sheepish as they settled themselves
on the crackly plastic of my sofa. Kelly Anne carefully removed

her mask, unclipped her handbag and applied lipstick as Darryl began to speak.

'Well. It's been a bit up and down since we last saw you.' He smiled but through the jollity I could see he was uncomfortable. 'All sorted now though, Susanna. I'm sorry if we put you through it a bit,' he laughed. 'We've kissed and made up!'

I waited but neither of them spoke. Eventually, I said, 'It seems your relationship can feel absolutely blissful and absolutely unbearable. I imagine these swings of feeling might be quite difficult to cope with.'

They looked at one another. Kelly Anne shrugged and said, 'I hate it, it's like we're driving each other crazy and Darryl *never* admits it's down to him too. He says it's all me, all my fault. I'm getting all the blame, but he provokes me . . . Yesterday, when we were supposed to be making dinner together, he spent over an hour on the phone to Natalie, sweet-talking her because she was having a hissy fit. I could hear him promising to take her out on Saturday, when we already have plans to play tennis with friends and . . .' She was in full flow now and the more she talked, the angrier she seemed to get. I watched as Darryl became increasingly agitated. His previous jollity evaporated, he frowned and looked away. I could see they were about to descend into something even more destructive, which would get us nowhere, so I interrupted her flow.

'Perhaps it would be helpful to widen the lens,' I suggested. They looked at me, not understanding. 'I've heard a bit about the current difficulties you're having but I don't feel I know much about either of you – I know how you met and a little about your previous relationships but nothing about your family backgrounds. We might be able to think together about what's at the heart of these upsetting feelings if we understand more about how you grew up?'

I knew that without more insight into their families I would continue to be lost at sea. I needed to get a sense of what they might be repeating and trying to resolve from their pasts if I was to begin to help them. I thought they might be reluctant to tell me much but Kelly Anne jumped in, saying, 'I'll go first.'

She told me that when she was small, she'd lived with her mother and grandmother in Kentucky, but at seven, she moved east with her mother, her mother's new boyfriend and his three children. She liked her stepbrother and kept in touch with him and his wife but she'd never got on with her stepsisters and she'd missed her grandmother a lot.

'My stepfather was a dictator, a complete control freak. We argued a lot. I left as soon as I could. At 17, I went back to Kentucky to live with my gramma and I went to college. I never went back home. My mom and stepdad were toxic together – they got divorced about ten years ago.'

'Toxic? In what way?' I asked. And then she told me that her stepfather had been quite weird. He was 'phobic' about everything and when she hit her teenage years, he got more odd and 'weird' with her. I looked at her questioningly but it was clear she didn't want to say any more.

'My real dad, he still lives near my gramma's house and I used to see him on the sidewalk from time to time – he'd wave at me. He was always in a bar and once we had a chat but I think it was mainly so I'd buy him a drink.' She grunted and sighed and made a dismissive gesture with her hand.

'You had a lot of disruptions in your childhood, Kelly Anne. It sounds like leaving your grandma was really painful?'

'Yeah. She's the only one of my family I've ever really been close to. She's 90 this year and in a retirement home and since I've been in London and what with Covid, I haven't seen her, not even once . . .' And she began to cry, tears slowly sliding down her cheeks. Darryl took her hand; she leant into him and he held her quietly for a moment.

I didn't say anything more then but I could sense my feelings towards her shifting because now I could relate to the child part of Kelly Anne and feel how complicated her life had been. As I entered her experience in my mind, I felt myself come alive with connections. How challenging it must have been to go from having your mum and grandma to yourself to suddenly losing one of the most important people in your life. And how hard it must have been for Kelly Anne to share her mum with her new stepfather *and* three other children. I began to feel more sympathy towards her difficulties with Natalie; maybe sharing Darryl with his children was just too much like a repeat of what she'd had to do in her childhood? We sat in silence as Kelly Anne recovered herself and then I turned to Darryl.

'And your family? Can you tell me a little?'

'What do you want to know?' Darryl asked. But I didn't get a chance to reply because he launched into the story of his life and there was no stopping him. He told me that he'd grown up in Inverness, that his father was a vet and his mother, a nurse. They were very religious and family life revolved round the Church. His mother favoured his older brother who was a star athlete and brilliant at school. His father, on the other hand, had favoured his younger sister, who'd also become a vet and taken over his father's practice. He said that he always knew that he wasn't going to get the attention that his brother and sister had but it was OK because he got a lot of freedom. They didn't really seem to expect much of him and hadn't complained when he decided to leave school at 16 and join the navy. He talked at length about what a great experience the navy was, how it had helped him to grow up and get the confidence he needed to start a business. Then he launched into his career and detailed his various achievements – the businesses he'd started and sold. He described the clever idea behind his present enterprise and where he was planning to take it. Gradually, I realised that what was happening in the room seemed to mirror the way he'd dealt with his past.

'I notice, Darryl, that you've skimmed over your childhood and quickly moved onto when you left home. It sounds that, like Kelly Anne, you had some quite challenging issues in your family and, like Kelly Anne, you got away from them as fast and as soon as you could. And now, here, talking to me, you've got away from thinking about the past as quickly as possible.'

He looked curious but said nothing, so I continued. 'Do you mind if we go back to your childhood, just for a bit? I feel I've only got a glimpse. How did your parents get on, for instance?'

'Oh Jesus,' he laughed. 'They hated each other. They couldn't even stand to be in the same room. They shouldn't have stayed together but, you know, they were really into the Church, so . . .' He shrugged, lifting his shoulders in resignation. 'My sister spent all her time with Dad and Mum was always with Douglas, my brother. Me? I stayed out of it. No one bothered me if I stayed out of the way.'

'You talk as if it were a breeze, as if this situation was actually good for you. But I wonder if somewhere you felt then, and perhaps can still do at times, quite neglected, left out?'

'Maybe . . .' he said politely but I could see he wasn't interested in delving deeper.

Despite that, I continued. 'Do you think that this feeling of not getting enough attention is one you both share? From what I heard, it sounds like Kelly Anne might have found it quite difficult to suddenly have to share her mother with a new stepfather and new step-siblings. And you, Darryl, you sound like you *never* felt you came first. It makes me wonder if some of the arguments about Natalie are because the two of you are finding it hard to share each other. You've only been together a short while and straight away you have to make room in your relationship for Natalie and Cathy. Maybe, Kelly Anne, it feels a bit too early to share Darryl with his children?'

They looked at each other and nodded and for a beat I thought we'd got somewhere, and this was a beginning. But a moment later, Darryl seemed to shake me off and said dismissively, 'Oh, I don't think either of us find sharing hard. We're both big givers, you know!' And he laughed and patted Kelly Anne's hand, telling her it was time to go.

After they left, I tried to put the pieces together. I could see that, on the surface, both had adopted a rather dismissive, 'who gives a shit' kind of persona. It was a brittle, hard shell around them and my attempts to get through it had been mostly without success. But both had described childhoods in which they'd been deprived of attention and I also thought that, perhaps, there was something darker lurking in Kelly Anne's experience that she'd shied away from talking about.

Could it be that closeness between fathers or father figures and daughters was stirring up something quite alarming for her? Was that why she was so hostile to the relationship between Darryl and his elder daughter? Was her concern about the way Natalie dressed also a clue? Something about Natalie's emerging sexuality was clearly bothering her.

I also wondered about *his* experience of always being left out in the family and how, now, that was exactly the experience that *Kelly Anne* was having with his daughters. Was he projecting his own competitive feelings into Kelly Anne? All the currents of their past lives, all their many fears and fantasies were driving the present difficulties between them. These unresolved issues had drawn this couple together and now these same things were driving them apart.

But I never got to find out if any of my speculations were, in any way, valid. They didn't turn up the following week, and when I contacted them to find out why, Kelly Anne said they'd split up again. I wrote back, encouraging them to come and explore whether this was what they really wanted. I heard nothing for three weeks and then I got a brief text from Darryl saying they'd started divorce proceedings – so thank you, but no thanks.

I think Darryl and Kelly Anne's difficulties probably ran quite deep but if they'd been able to stay the course, I think I might have helped them. Their marriage seemed to have been about an escape – from their previous relationships and from the pain of their pasts. They'd got together in a whirl, creating an illusion that everything could be left behind and nothing painful needed to be confronted and mourned.

Making changes and facing the ghosts that haunt and shape our lives is hard to do and most of us find ways not to look too deep. It seems we prefer to swipe right, get a new lover, have a drink, buy a new dress or simply turn a blind eye. Our society encourages us to move fast because moving slow costs money. Even our NHS mental health services love a quick CBT 'fix' despite its abject failure to 'fix' many people at all. Instead, patients go round and round and round the system, seeking desperately for something that short-term therapy can't provide.

From childhood, Kelly Anne and Darryl had found a way to deal with their hurt and pain: they simply moved on. And now they were doing it again, moving on from each other and from me. And, without a backward glance, that was that.

REGGIE AND LAWRENCE PLAY PIGGY IN THE MIDDLE

As soon as Reggie and Lawrence began to talk, I felt optimistic that I could help them. They'd come, they quickly reassured me, not because they'd had any problems of their own but because they were concerned that their 25-year-old son seemed stuck.

'Stuck?' I enquired.

'Yes, stuck at home,' said Lawrence. 'I think even Reggie thinks it's time he moved on.' Reggie, with a resigned sigh, nodded her head in agreement.

As they told me more about their son, Woody, I gradually noticed how difficult it was to focus on them both. They were sitting as far apart on my couch as they could possibly get and, as they talked, I felt like a spectator at Wimbledon, my head turning from side to side as each of them played their shot. Often, they interrupted each other and disagreed, eager to tell me their 'true' version of events. By the end of the first session, I felt exhausted. Despite this tiredness, however, I had a good feeling that they'd found the session useful. They needed a lot of support but I was hopeful I could assist them and thereby help Woody to get on with his life.

At the next session, they again sat far apart. Underneath her taupe trench coat, I could see that Reggie was wearing stripy tights and an orange corduroy dress. Her colourful clothes made her look a little like a presenter on a children's television programme. Lawrence was dressed like a farmer – thick brown trousers and a rough, tweedy jacket covering his Tattersall shirt. He was clean-shaven but his long, thinning hair was pushed back off his face and rested gently on his shoulders. They told me they were gardeners and you could see from their ruddy faces and weather-beaten hands that they spent a lot of time outdoors.

'I'd like to say, Susanna, how helpful the last meeting was. I really felt you "got" the issues and, after we got home, I had a long talk with Woody that evening, which felt like a bit of a breakthrough.'

As soon as he drew breath, Reggie interrupted Lawrence's flow. 'I didn't know you spoke to Woody last week. You didn't say. *I* spoke to him too. On Friday. When did *you* speak to him? Was it before or after?'

'What does it matter?' Lawrence snapped, raising his hands in the air in a gesture of exasperation. He turned to me and, in a much more reasonable voice, proceeded to tell me how he felt he'd really connected with Woody and how Woody had agreed that he'd do more in the house and perhaps come and help them on some jobs, once he finished his dissertation.

'His dissertation?' I enquired.

'You did what?' Reggie said, ignoring me. 'Why'd you say he could work with us? You know he hates gardening and how does it help him become more independent if he's working for us? It doesn't, does it?'

This back and forth continued at pace and I had to work overtime to manage the session in such a way that each of them had a say. Each of my interventions seemed to chime with them and I found myself liking them a great deal; their passion and engagement was evident. On the other hand, I confess to feeling irritated with Woody – he sounded rather selfish, lazy and entitled. He needs a firmer approach, I thought to myself, but it was clear that Reggie and Lawrence seemed to be set on taking it in turns to protect him in one way or another.

The following session, they arrived wearing heavy boots covered in mud, which they proceeded to unlace and leave by the door, padding over to the couch in their socks. Reggie spoke first, smiling at me and asking how I was.

'I'd like to talk about what happened on Tuesday evening,' she said, glancing at Lawrence, who nodded his assent. 'I think it would be helpful because it was a really good example of what goes on with Woody all the time.'

'Was it Tuesday?' Lawrence suddenly interrupted. 'I think it was Wednesday, when we got back from Kingston.'

'It doesn't matter which day,' Reggie said coldly, raising her eyebrows in contempt and looking to me for agreement.

Before they started their usual bickering I interrupted. 'Shall we stay with what you were going to tell me? I think you both wanted me to hear it.' And they nodded in agreement. Lawrence was about to speak but Reggie shushed him with a fierce look and took up the reins.

'We'd just got back. From Kingston. We've been working on a big project down there, a great project, actually. I was knackered, we both were. And, as usual, Woody was in the dining room playing on his Xbox and the kitchen was ab-so-lute-ly *filthy*! He'd obviously been in there all day; there were cups, plates, glasses. And he'd been smoking – you could smell it. And I said to him, quite nicely, "Please clear up."'

Lawrence huffed dismissively.

'I did say it nicely,' Reggie responded, turning on Lawrence.

'I didn't say anything!'

And then they were off again, bickering about Woody's attitude and how Reggie's version of what happened was entirely wrong or entirely right.

I put up my hand. 'Stop! Let's just try to think through

together what happened.' And they both looked at me guilt-
ily and quietened down.

'I don't want to start another fight but really, Lawrie,
why won't you ever support me? We make an agreement –
we'd agreed, hadn't we? That we'd ask him to help out more
but then as soon as I challenge him, you jump in to defend
him. Why? You make it seem like I'm being a bitch . . . or
something. I don't think I am.'

'You jump on him; you know what you do. Like he's like
minding his own business and you're on him as soon as we
walk in. I don't know, it just seems you don't give him a
chance. And then you're on at *me* for not doing something or
other, or not being *supportive*,' Lawrence finished, spitting
out the last word contemptuously.

'Is it ever the other way round?' I asked.

They looked at me puzzled.

'Is it ever Reggie saying that *you're* being too tough, too
harsh? Is it ever that way round?'

'Sometimes . . . yes,' Lawrence replied hesitantly. 'Not so
much recently but definitely when he was younger. You never
let me tell him off . . . ever. *Ever!* Not when he was little –
no way! You're just as bad as me,' Lawrence concluded
triumphantly.

They continued to rant at each other about who'd been
the most involved and who'd been most devoted when Woody
was younger. I was wondering where this would take us when
Reggie began to speak in a different tone.

'What you don't know, Susanna, is that I was actually
pregnant before Woody, about a year before he was born. I
had a late miscarriage.'

'It was a stillbirth, Reg, wasn't it? Not really a miscarriage,' Lawrence interjected.

And then they told me about the son they'd lost, just a
month before he was due to be born. They never found out

why he'd died; the pregnancy had gone smoothly and they were both so happy and then suddenly he stopped moving. As they spoke, they seemed to relive the horror of it. Reggie sobbed and Lawrence stared glassily into the distance, and I felt tears welling in my eyes too. But after the session ended, I also wondered why Reggie had called it a miscarriage. Did it sound less traumatic? More 'normal', somehow?

As the weeks went by, it became clearer they *both* struggled to be firm with Woody. We talked about how these parenting difficulties were very much shared, as they took it in turns to admonish and then indulge him. Reggie would often scold him for not doing something in the house or nag him about his coursework, but then a heartbeat later, she'd be making him a snack or doing his laundry and paying his mobile bill.

At some point, as almost always happens when couples come to discuss problems with their children, Reggie and Lawrence stopped talking about Woody and started talking about themselves. There was a painful disappointment with their sex life, which had dwindled away and now they were never intimate with each other. It was unclear why they'd stopped having sex as each of them declared they missed it. Despite this, neither of them was able to take the initiative. Neither would, in the quiet, dark of the night, make the move towards the other. It was as though they were frozen, full of longing but petrified, like marble sarcophagi in their bed.

Though I could sense their discomfort, I decided to be more direct about their lack of love-making. I asked when it had begun to fade and whether they had thoughts about why this had happened. At this point, they started to find it problematic to attend together. One week, Lawrence had such a bad back that he couldn't come. The next, Reggie had to visit her mother. Then Lawrence had a dental appointment, which couldn't be rearranged, and Reggie had to take Woody to a job interview. So it went on, with me seeing each of them in turn and I confess it took me some weeks to make the link, that exploring their sex life jointly was something they were, unconsciously, resisting.

It was November and freezing cold when I finally got them back in the room together. The heating in my office had broken down so we were making do with a noisy and only partly effective blow heater.

'Woody's got a job!' Lawrence told me excitedly.

'He's working for Help the Aged,' Reggie chimed in, laughing.

'Feel sorry for the aged,' Lawrence joked.

And then they competed to tell me more about the news and, once again, I felt my head turning repeatedly from side to side as I tried to listen to them both equally. And then, as usual, they fell to bickering.

'I don't know why *you're* even talking about it to Susanna. You were against him having a job until he got his MA,' Lawrence said angrily.

'Rubbish, *I* took him for the interview,' Reggie said petulantly, glancing at me. '*I* helped with the application. You really think *you're* the only one who does anything for Woody?'

'You're *always* jealous of our relationship. Always. You never let me and Woody have a moment. It's not all about you. You really know how to spoil things.'

Suddenly, it occurred to me. I was Woody. Or rather, there was something similar in the way they related to me and him. They competed over me in the same way they competed over their son. It was happening right now. As they argued, both were keeping one eye on how I was reacting, whose side I would come down on, and I was finding myself having that old familiar 'Wimbledon' feeling as I struggled to listen and attend to them both.

'It seems you both feel that Woody doesn't have a

relationship with the two of you as a couple. And that means you have to compete for his love. I wonder if you feel similarly with me – you're both constantly checking which of you I really like better? I think you believe that only one of you can get my attention, my care, and that the other is then going to be completely left out in the cold. As if you can't imagine that I can hold you both in mind?'

They stopped bickering and turned to reassuring me that it wasn't so. They both thought I was entirely fair, they said, and this was one of the reasons they felt safe with me. But something clearly chimed with them as they then began to explore their competitiveness. They laughed as they recounted how they behaved when they played games and they acknowledged they could turn everything into a race.

'When you were kids, did you compete with your siblings?' I asked.

'My sister was so much older that I felt more like an only child. I was definitely my father's favourite, wasn't I?' Reggie began, looking to Lawrence for confirmation. 'He always took my side. If Mum was cross, he'd always tell her off. Since he died, I've got much closer to my mum.' Reggie paused. 'I felt . . . feel . . . a bit guilty about how I treated her when I was a teenager.' I watched her absorb what she'd just said. 'I'd hate to think I was doing the same with Woody . . . I don't want him to feel "piggy in the middle" like I did.'

'Piggy in the middle?' I echoed, seeking more.

'Yes, well, they were always fighting. My mum was always on at my dad about something or other. Usually money,' she said ruefully. 'I think *I* felt sorry for him and, because she nagged me too, *he* felt sorry for me.'

'It sounds like you and your father had some kind of special bond?' I ventured. She nodded. 'Which excluded your mother,' I continued.

She nodded again and then noticed how perplexed

Lawrence looked. She turned her hand in that familiar short-hand for the question 'What?'

'But your dad loved your mother; he was devoted to her. I never saw them argue. They seemed . . . tight, very close. At least, to me.'

'That was after, after I left home. I think it changed once I moved out. You didn't see them before. There's a before and after. They fought like cat and dog.'

We talked more about Reggie's childhood and how she was sorry she never really had a sister or brother around and then, suddenly, they began to talk about the lost baby. I'd almost forgotten about the stillbirth – it had been so many months since we'd discussed it – but now it seemed very important.

'I wish we'd had two children. One isn't quite enough to go round,' Lawrence said, laughing ruefully. And then he talked about what it had been like for him growing up with five brothers and sisters: an experience so markedly different to Reggie's. 'It was great in lots of ways. I was never alone. I always had someone to play with . . . or fight with. I've always thought it's a bit sad for Woody, he's just got us . . .'

'But I guess it must've been hard at times to get attention?' I commented. 'Attention from your parents for instance?'

'Kinda,' Lawrence replied, looking thoughtful.

It was the end of the session and it felt as though we'd got somewhere. Where, I wasn't sure, but something was shifting. I knew that for this couple, the issues they struggled with circled around the problem of threesomes. It was as though they really believed the old adage, 'Two's company and three's a crowd.' A crowd in which you were unlikely to get seen or noticed.

The weeks passed and Reggie and Lawrence made slow and steady progress. They continued to bicker about who was doing what and whether Woody was pulling his weight but their fighting seemed less vicious and we had more and more reflective moments. I had the feeling that Woody was also doing better; the old arguments about him had lessened. He seemed to have a girlfriend, Maya, though neither Reggie nor Lawrence was permitted to meet her, but it was clear he was out and about more and no longer always stuck at home on his Xbox.

Then, one week they came in and I knew immediately that something was wrong.

Neither of them spoke for quite some time; they avoided looking at each other and even at me. We sat in silence, the clock's ticking the only accompaniment to the deepening quiet. From outside, I could hear the sounds of children coming out of the school opposite my house.

'Difficult to start today?' I eventually commented.

Nothing. We sat longer and I could feel the tension rising. After a while, I tried again. 'Perhaps you're both too upset to talk?'

This seemed to stir Reggie, who looked at me as if noticing my presence for the first time. She smiled gently and I thought she was trying to apologise for their lack of response.

'I guess we should explain.' Lawrence's voice almost made me jump as it punctured the heavy silence. Then he told me that there'd been an almighty row the previous evening, which had culminated in Woody packing his bags and moving out. They weren't sure where he'd gone but they thought it was probably to his girlfriend's. Then they became animated and talked anxiously for some minutes about what they should do. They'd tried his mobile numerous times but it was switched off and they'd rung some of his friends but they didn't seem to know where he was. They didn't have Maya's number, nor did they know where she lived. As they talked, I could feel the fear rising and, as it did, they became angrier and blaming.

'If he doesn't come back, I'll never forgive you,' Reggie spat.

'I won't be your whipping boy. You're not going to do the usual – make it all my fault. You were the one on his back – not me. As usual. If you hadn't gone on about the mess in the car, he wouldn't have left. But you just couldn't shut up. He'd already done a lot.'

'He hadn't done a lot, that's total rubbish. You want me to look after YOU *and* you want me to look after him. What am I? Mummy to you both? He doesn't need me to mummy him anymore – isn't that what we've been agreeing with Susanna? But he does need you to step up and be a proper father for Christ's sake. Set an example, stop whining to me!'

They made little progress that session and when they left in high dudgeon, I felt worried about them. That night, I woke in the early hours of the morning, wondering where Woody had got to and whether he was safe.

Weeks passed and Woody didn't come back and nor did he contact them. He didn't answer their messages or pick up his phone; he completely shut them out. I watched them break and it was heart-rending. Session after session, they'd weep and fight and weep and fight and all I could do was be with them in their anger and grief. Many times, I held back my own tears as they tried to come to terms with Woody's absence. They knew he was safe; they'd heard from one of his friends that he was around and fine, living with Maya in south London. They could also see what he was posting on his social media accounts but he'd changed his phone number and didn't respond to emails. He'd left them, abandoned them, and it felt a cruel and bitter way to leave.

I told them that I thought Woody had felt this was the only way to separate from them, that he'd had to mobilise every bit of anger he felt to tear himself from their soft bosom. Maybe that thought helped them a little, I'm not really sure. Lawrence couldn't sleep and the doctor prescribed sleeping pills; Reggie found it difficult to get out of bed in the mornings and the doctor prescribed anti-depressants. They were powerless to do anything and had no choice but to wait and hope and I waited and hoped with them.

Sometimes, of course, they hated their son but it never lasted long. They reserved their deepest anger for Maya, who they decided was a witch, a bitch and worse for stealing Woody. I tried to help them see that Woody was grown and had made his own choices; for all they knew, Maya could be appealing to him to contact them.

For some couples, this might have brought them together but Woody had been the glue between them; without him there, what was left? They began to talk about separation, Reggie leading the way. She decided she didn't want to work with Lawrence anymore, that she was too old for gardening, and took a job working for a friend in a local bookshop. Lawrence sulked, retreating to the office shed, where, hour after hour, he played his guitar and kept out of Reggie's way. Their nest had emptied and they were now faced with just each other and what was left between them.

There are many couples who, once they have children, lose their connection to each other. Often, this problem is linked to a feeling that intimacy between them is cruelly excluding for the children; where there is only one child, this problem can be worse. Family life becomes centred around the child and their needs but once they leave home (and in this situation, children can take a whole lot longer to do that), the couple find themselves without a relationship to fall back on.

Though I tried hard, during this period I felt I couldn't reach either Lawrence or Reggie; the wound they'd suffered was scarring over and they now seemed resigned that their marriage was over too. They blamed each other for what had happened, shoving the guilt and sense of failure out of themselves into each other. They forgot what they'd shared, the life they'd built. In the sessions, they'd often reconnect but it was as if being together without Woody was too painful to bear. Nearly a year after Woody fled, Lawrence moved out to stay with his sister, Iris.

Despite their separation, they continued to come to see me. I think I was, at that point, an anchor of sorts, in a darkening sea. Perhaps I linked them back to hope, to love and to each other?

Then, three weeks after Lawrence moved out, Woody turned up at Reggie's door, suitcase in hand. I was fascinated by this; it seemed extraordinary that Woody would come back just as Lawrence left. What did it mean? Was it the threesome that Woody hadn't been able to stand anymore? Was that why he'd left? Did Lawrence's absence now leave a space for Woody to occupy, allowing him to have Reggie all to himself? Was it simply that now he wouldn't have to be 'piggy in the middle'? Or was it that he felt he couldn't leave his poor mother on her own?

On a bright, crisp Monday morning in April, two weeks later, Reggie and Lawrence arrived together for their session. I could hear them chatting and laughing as they came through the gate and I smiled to myself, wondering if a rapprochement was now under way.

There was no hesitation today as Lawrence pulled off his battered khaki parka. 'We've had a good week. Lots to tell you.' He glanced at Reggie who nodded in agreement. 'We talked to Woody properly. It was awkward but really, really helpful. I feel sooo relieved and you do too, don't you, Reg?'

'Yeah, yeah. Shall I tell her what he said?'

'Absolutely,' Lawrence answered. I was struck by how

they finally seemed to be acting like a couple. 'Well, we talked for hours last Tuesday – it was . . . amazing. I can't tell you, Susanna. It felt like . . . being reborn,' Reggie laughed. 'What you said last week about us needing to sit down as a family really helped. After seeing you, we went for lunch and agreed we couldn't let him "split" us, you know, like you described, how we needed to be a team. You saying, "Remember you're on the same team" really rang a bell for us. Because that's always been the problem, hasn't it? Not knowing we were on the same side. So we went home and told him we wanted to talk to him. He looked really scared and I was scared too. I thought he might run away again.'

'I went home for dinner the next night,' Lawrence now took up the reins excitedly. 'I was shitting myself, to be frank, but Woody said he was sorry. He'd just needed to get away for a bit because he was fed up with us.'

'Was he able to tell you what he was fed up about?' I asked.

'Us rowing. Rowing and . . . nagging,' Lawrence replied. 'He said there was no room for him. Which is ironic. That we were fighting over him all the time but he never got to speak.'

'Yes, and about us being too focused on the business,' Reggie added.

'Well, a bit. But that wasn't the main thing. It was us rowing wasn't it?'

I could see they were about to squabble and I pointed out the irony of this, which made us all laugh. I thought about how, on numerous occasions, I'd probably had a similar experience to that which Woody had lived with daily. I felt torn between them, which made me kind of important too because they both wanted my approval and attention. But I'd also often felt powerless; their competitiveness made them so totally focused on each other that there seemed to be no room for anyone else. Except, perhaps, as a referee to their battles? I thought about the loneliness of that for a child and the invidious situation of being that 'piggy in the middle'. Woody had clearly felt neglected and, in leaving, he'd made *them* feel as neglected and overlooked as he'd felt himself.

Much changed after that. We did the work of understanding all these disparate threads and they began to acknowledge how difficult it was for Woody as well as for them to be in this threesome. In their inner worlds, there always seemed a danger that someone would be left out and they fought over who that would be. Each, in competing to be the best and most loved by Woody, would indulge him. But in fighting to win, Woody's real emotional needs were overlooked. And no one won.

In a session not long before they stopped coming, Reggie spoke about how she'd felt anxious having sex with Lawrence ever since Woody was a baby. She worried he'd wake up and need them and they wouldn't hear him when he cried. We explored how, deep down, they'd felt guilty about being intimate, sexually or in any way, because then they'd be excluding Woody. These Oedipal dynamics permeated the family system, shaping everything.

Then Woody moved out again to live with a friend and almost immediately Lawrence moved back in. He stayed in the spare room and both of them seemed comfortable with that. It seemed they needed to be more separate. When they ended the therapy, it was with a quiet gratitude. I thought they'd grown up a lot; they were both much more subdued, they fought much less – but then, perhaps, they shared less too?

All couples must learn to accept the limitations of their relationship. Some couples try to manage their disappointments by avoiding things or finding comfort elsewhere. Other couples, like Reggie and Lawrence, seem to engage in a long, passionate battle to get what they want and, in some way, these battles keep couples very absorbed with each other. Most couples, as the years pass, stop *most* of the fighting. The natural processes of ageing make us more aware of the cost of conflict and, battle-worn, we slowly accept who our partner is and recognise that some things simply are as they are. Because of this, couples lower their expectations of each other and when that happens, there is less disappointment and more capacity to enjoy and appreciate what they have.

POSTSCRIPT

Many readers may find aspects of these cases frustrating. They may wish for more detail, more clarity and especially clearer and more certain outcomes. I am sorry for this but I can only say it is the same frustration that every psychoanalytic therapist lives with every day. One can never actually know the unconscious – if one could, it wouldn't be unconscious, would it? All we can hope to do is take some soundings from the deep and learn to notice the waving flags that appear on the surface from time to time. Understanding is always speculation and only meaningful if it is meaningful to the patient.

So many of these chapters end without any conclusion, the patients simply falling off the page and out of sight. I can't apologise for this lack – it is exactly what I experience. I very rarely know if the therapy has led to a couple or an individual patient having a good-enough life. I don't find out if a couple stayed together or if their children thrived. It is unfortunate but it keeps me, as much as possible, in the now and that is where feelings – the essential business of therapy – usually live. So, in order to be authentic, I'm afraid you have to cope without much of an end to the story, just as I do.

Much of this book was written during the pandemic and it is clear that this global disaster has had an enormous impact on us all and on our family life. I don't think anyone can quite know as yet what that impact means, though we are all keen to jump to conclusions. How we have fared psychologically isn't known, though the impact on children and adolescents is beginning to look worrying.

What I have noticed is that for some couples, the pandemic has hardly been mentioned. The more distressed the couple, the less the pandemic seems to come into the sessions. I've begun to conclude that for most distressed patients, the inner world of feelings makes such a racket that the clamour and noise of the outside world makes hardly a sound.

ACKNOWLEDGEMENTS

I'd like to thank a lot of people. I have many, many people to be grateful to. Firstly, I must say thank you to my editor, Drummond Moir, who showed such confidence in me, despite my uncertainty about writing, and whose feedback and suggestions for the book have been invaluable. Acknowledgements are due to Liz Marvin for her skilful editing and to Jessica Patel for her help. Many thanks too to my agent, Zoe Ross. My colleagues at Queen Anne Street Practice, Biddy Arnott, Stephen Blumenthal and Susan Austin, have been such a huge, unfailing support through some tough times. They've cheered me on and provided wise advice. I'm grateful to Brett Kahr, Susie Orbach and Stephen Grosz, who all spoke to me when I began writing and gave freely of their time and experience. Brett's advice to write as if I was talking (I'm quite a good talker!) made such a difference to my confidence. Thanks to Jan McGregor Hepburn for her loving support. I am indebted to Alan Colam and David Hewison who discussed ethical matters with me. Vanessa Milton at Penguin Random House knows what she did and I cannot thank her enough.

I am deeply indebted to many of my colleagues and teachers at Tavistock Relationships, some of whom are sadly now dead. There are so many colleagues who have been inspirational and important to me that it's hard to list them all, but this book stands on their shoulders and couldn't have been written without them. Particular thanks must go to Warren Colman, Christopher Clulow, Mary Morgan, Stan Ruszczynski, David Hewison, Christel Buss-Twachtmann and Anton Obholzer. And a dedication in remembrance is due to James Fisher and Nina Cohen. All of these people were essential to my development as a psychoanalytic psycho-therapist and many of the ideas in this book come directly from their mouths. A long overdue thanks is also due to Eliza-beth Gee.

Thank you to my good friends who've listened to me bang on about this book for too long. Particularly to Profes-sor Lynda Nead, Charlotte Wickers, Jenny Riddell and Andrea Collett. And thanks must go to my sister Keren Abse for her generous support. Her home in Ogmore-by-Sea was such a welcome writing retreat.

Thank you to my husband, Paul Gogarty, without whom there simply wouldn't be a book. He must have read all the chapters a dozen times, editing my clumsy language, offering insight and imagination and correcting my appalling punctu-ation and making everything work so much better. To Miren Lopategui and Nigel Richardson – I am eternally grateful for your sharp eyes and thoughtful reading of the book.

And to my children, Max Gogarty and Larne Abse Gog-arty, and their spouses, Suzy Gregg and Adam Lane, who have been excited and patient with my bookishness. Finally, to my grandson, Rudy, who was born in the same week that I finally birthed this book. Your imminent arrival spurred me on to the finish line.

And lastly, but most definitely not least, a deep and enduring gratitude is owed to my patients past and present who have allowed me into their lives and from whom I've learnt so much.

O

20.99

31513500115493

CLACKMANNANSHIRE COUNCIL

bo~' is to be returned~ n or he' ...st date stamped below.

WITHDRAWN